# FAT QUARTER
# CHRISTMAS

# FAT QUARTER
# CHRISTMAS

25 projects to make from short lengths of fabric

Jemima Schlee

First published 2017 by
Guild of Master Craftsman Publications Ltd
Castle Place, 166 High Street, Lewes,
East Sussex, BN7 1XU, UK

Text © Jemima Schlee, 2017
Copyright in the Work © GMC Publications Ltd, 2017

ISBN 978 1 78494 353 0

While every effort has been made to obtain permission from
the copyright holders for all material used in this book, the
publishers will be pleased to hear from anyone who has not
been appropriately acknowledged and to make the correction
in future reprints.

The publishers and author can accept no legal responsibility
for any consequences arising from the application of
information, advice or instructions given in this publication.

A catalogue record for this book is available from the
British Library.

**Publisher** Jonathan Bailey
**Production Manager** Jim Bulley
**Senior Project Editor** Sara Harper
**Editor** Robin Pridy
**Managing Art Editor** Gilda Pacitti
**Art Editor** Luana Gobbo
**Photographer** Emma Sekhon
**Step photography** Jemima Schlee
**Picture credit** Cover illustrations: Shutterstock/Ohn Mar

Colour origination by GMC Reprographics
Printed and bound in Malaysia

## A note on measurements

The imperial measurements in these projects are
converted from metric. While every attempt has
been made to ensure that they are as accurate
as possible, some rounding up or down has been
inevitable. For this reason, it is always best to
stick to one system or the other throughout
a project: do not mix metric and imperial units.

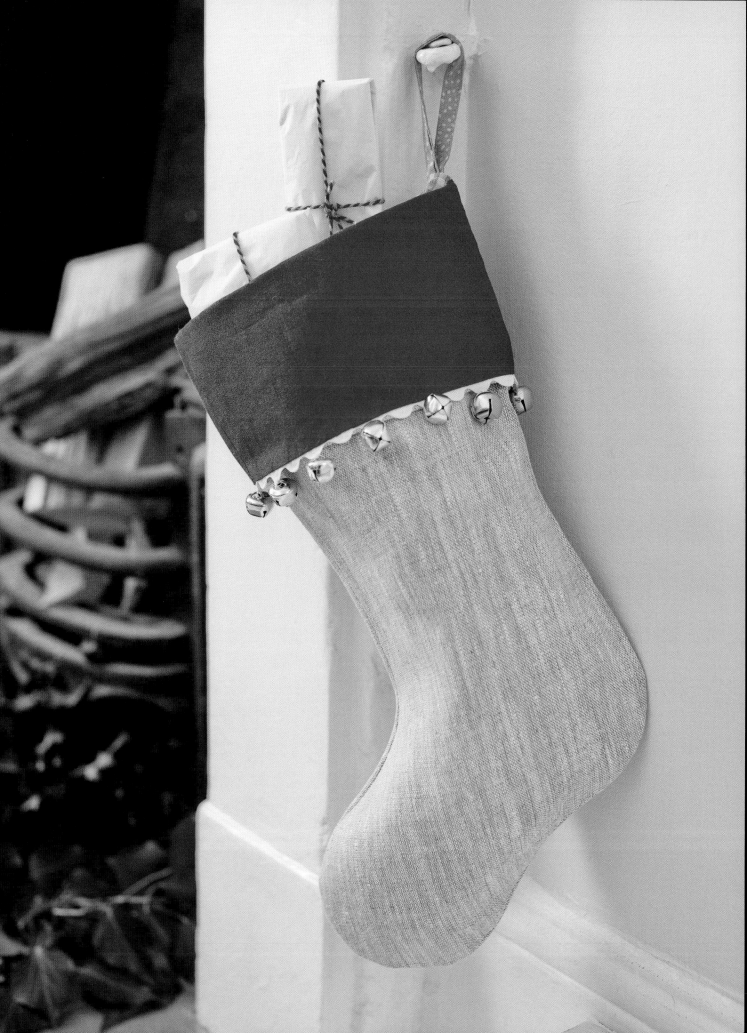

# CONTENTS

# INTRODUCTION

I have all sorts of fabrics in myriad colours tucked away: small pieces stored within a chest of drawers, larger pieces stowed in vintage suitcases. From fat quarters I've been unable to resist buying, to remnants left over from dress-making projects, vintage garments that evoke precious childhood memories and eclectic fabric scraps, there are always new additions to my stash. If, like me, you can't bear to throw fabrics away, then you too are bound to have a selection of fabulous offcuts and oddments of material just crying out to be used.

Here are 25 stylish and festive projects to help you to make the most of these pieces of fabric. Making Christmas accessories and decorations is a perfect way to transform some of these treasured textiles into gorgeous items to embellish your home or to give as special presents. Each can either be made from fabric scraps, or remnants pieced together, or specially purchased fat quarters. A fat quarter is simply half a yard of fabric cut in half again vertically, and in this book it refers to an 18 x 22in (46 x 56cm) maximum piece of fabric. Sizes do vary, depending upon the width from which the fabric is cut, so bear this in mind when working out your fabric requirements. The style of a project is dictated by your fabric choice, and colour and pattern can completely alter its character. Choose traditional red and white, or mix colours that pop – remember, you can make these projects year after year to go with new colour schemes if you wish.

Creating your own accessories and decorations adds a very personal touch to your Christmas. Stockings last for a childhood, and maybe beyond; napkin rings and tea-light holders can be remade in different colours and fabric each holiday, while adding a handful of new ornaments to your tree each year results in a wonderful collection before very long. Using beautiful fabrics to make personalized crafted projects makes the whole process even more satisfying. Most of the projects are very quick and easy to make, and you will only need basic sewing skills and a sewing machine. You'll be amazed at how creative you can be with just a few small pieces of fabric.

*Jemima*

# THE BASICS

# MATERIALS & EQUIPMENT

Each project in this book lists all the tools and equipment you will need. For most projects, you will need a sewing machine and thread, a sewing needle, pins, sharp dress-making scissors, a pen or fabric marker and an iron. Here are some tips for storing and using your tools and equipment.

**THREADS** Cotton thread is strong and firm, and comes in an infinite variety of colours. Large jam jars store hand- and machine-sewing threads effectively, especially when grouped in colours, reducing tangles and speeding up the search for a specific shade.

**PINS AND PINNING** Pinning and tacking ensures the fabric will not slip about when stitching, producing a straight, neat seam. Pins with coloured glass heads are easy to find in fabric. Place pins at right angles to the stitching line if machine stitching over them to avoid having to tack or baste.

**NEEDLES** Sharps have a relatively large eye, making them fairly easy to thread for hand stitching. Embroidery needles are thicker and have a larger eye to accommodate the thicker embroidery thread.

**MEASURING** Whether using a measuring tape or a ruler, be sure to consistently use either imperial or metric measurements – never mix the two.

**BOBBINS** If sewing two different-coloured fabrics together, to make stitching less visible, it can be useful to sew with one colour threaded on the machine needle, and another colour in the bobbin. For this, it is very important to keep stitch tension even so that the different colours are not pulled through to the other side of the fabric.

Keep little pillboxes of fully charged bobbins in a variety of colours – this way you can pop in a fresh, full bobbin when you've run out, rather than having to unthread and thread the machine to fill one.

**IRON** It makes all the difference to the finish of a project to iron as you go along, ironing after you have completed each step.

**FABRICS** Choose natural fibres whenever possible, such as linens, cottons or linen/cotton mixes. You can mix and match oddments to make up the amounts required for the project, but choose fabrics of similar weights. Most of these projects are fairly small and heavyweight fabrics are not suitable as seams and corners become bulky and hard to work with. Natural fibres are best washed before to avoid problems with shrinkage later. For trims and ties use simple, traditional rickrack, piping cord, herringbone and woven tapes, 100% cotton threads and plain buttons in coordinating colours.

**SCISSORS** Ideally, you should have two pairs of sewing scissors. A small pair of sharp, pointed scissors is essential for cutting threads and trimming corners and curves. Then you need a pair of sewing shears. These have long blades and a bent handle so that the scissors can rest on the table while cutting, keeping the fabric flat. The blades should be kept sharp. Make sure your scissors are used solely for fabrics so that no one uses them to cut paper.

**SEAM RIPPER** A seam ripper is used for unpicking stitches. Insert the pointed blade underneath the thread to be cut. Push it forward against the thread and the blade will cut it. When all the stitches have been removed, the seam can be re-sewn. It's possible to run the blade along a line of stitching between the two layers of fabric and cut all the stitches in one movement, but it takes a bit of skill to prevent tearing.

# TECHNIQUES

The projects in this book mostly involve basic sewing techniques, both by hand and machine. All the information to complete the projects is given here, including basic instructions and some specific tips to help your sewing go smoothly.

## PREPARING TO SEW

Here are a few pointers for choosing and organising a workspace. Whether you are using a temporary space, or lucky enough to have an area dedicated to making and sewing, it is best to be well organized, and finding good storage and lighting is essential.

### YOUR WORKSPACE

Be sure to work in a well-lit environment. If natural lighting is on the gloomy side, use a lamp – preferably a directional and adjustable one – to enhance the situation. If right-handed, have a lamp to your left (and vice versa), thus avoiding working in the shadow of your leading hand. If you are lucky enough to have a dedicated workspace, keep an ironing board and iron at the ready. If space is limited, iron with a folded towel or piece of thick fabric on the corner of the work surface to save space.

### USING TEMPLATES AND PATTERNS

If a project uses a simple square, rectangle or circle of fabric, the dimensions of these are given within the project instructions. All other templates are on pages 138–149. These can be traced using tracing paper or baking parchment, or photocopied. In some cases, they may need enlarging – this can easily be done with a photocopier or scanner, or even by hand if the shapes are regular and you are particularly confident! Be sure to cut these templates out with paper-cutting scissors and not your fabric-cutting scissors.

### WINDOW TEMPLATES

This is, in effect, a 'negative' of a template or pattern piece. Cut the template shape out of the centre of a piece of blank paper. Use the hole created to choose which part of the fabric pattern or the pieced patchwork to use before marking the fabric and cutting it out.

## MARKING FABRIC

There are several ways to transfer templates and mark the fabric for cutting or stitching.

Tailor's chalk can be brushed away. Use a white one on dark cloth and a coloured one on lighter fabrics. It should be kept sharp to produce a clean and accurate line.

An air-erasable pen is very easy to use. Most fade after a couple of hours – do check though, as some need washing out.

Using a writing pen or a pencil is sometimes preferable – inevitably, raw edges are lost within seams or folded within hems, so any drawn lines will not be visible once the project is finished. A white pen can be handy for darker fabrics.

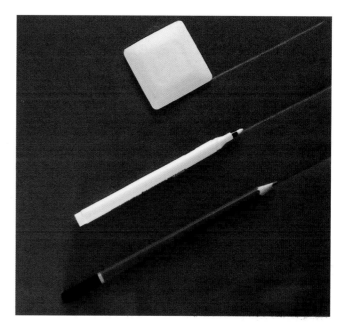

## INTERFACING AND STABILIZERS

You can buy fabric stiffeners in many weights. An iron-on version can be preferable because it reduces the number of layers to work with once it's fused to a piece of fabric. Use a hot iron to fix the stiffener to the wrong side of the fabric – read the manufacturer's instructions, as some require steam to fix them firmly. The most important thing is to check and double-check that the stiffener is glue side down before pressing it – cleaning glue off an iron isn't fun.

## IRONING

Have all ironing equipment set up and ready to use, near the workspace. The iron should have adjustable heat settings and a steam option that produces the right amount of moisture to make a crisp edge and flat seam. Steam scalds easily, however, so mind your fingers. Be sure to press each completed seam. Projects will indicate whether you need to press a seam to one side (A) or to press it open (B). Use the point of the iron to open seams.

## HAND STITCHES

Hand stitching is best used for temporary sewing (tacking and gathering), and finishing (hems and closing turning gaps).

### TACKING AND GATHERING

Tacking, also known as basting, is a line of temporary stitches used to fix pieces of fabric in position ready for permanent stitching. This is the easiest and quickest hand-sewing stitch. Knot the end of the thread and push the needle through from the back of the fabric to the front. Push the needle tip through to the back $^3/8$in (1cm) from the place it emerged, then out again to the front of your fabric $^3/8$in (1cm) further along. Pull the needle and thread through and repeat. Finish with a couple of stitches worked over each other to secure the end. When the seam or hem has been permanently sewn by machine, remove the tacking. Making your tacking stitch length shorter creates running stitch, which is very useful for gathering frills.

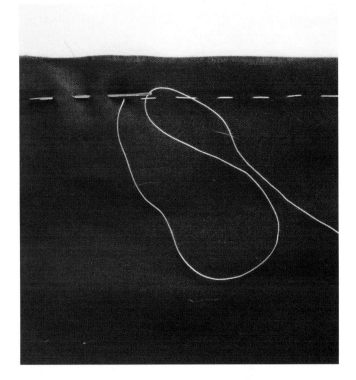

### OVERSTITCH

Use overstitch for closing turning gaps. With two pieces of fabric pinned or tacked together, or simply aligned, bring the needle up from within one folded edge to the front of the work. Now push the needle back through the folded edges of both pieces of fabric at a slight angle, catching a few threads of fabric from each. Pull the needle and thread through and repeat, spacing stitches $^1/8$–$^1/4$in (3–6mm) apart.

### HEM STITCH

Similar to overstitch, this stitch is used for hand-stitching hems. With the hem pinned or tacked, bring the needle up from within the hem's folded edge. Push the needle through the back layer of fabric, catching a few threads before bringing it back through the fold at the top of the hem. Pull the needle and thread through and repeat, spacing stitches $^1/8$–$^1/4$in (3–6mm) apart.

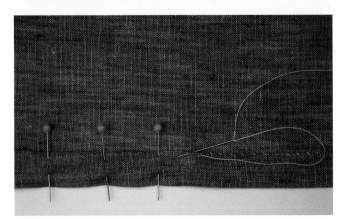

## BLANKET STITCH

This is traditionally used to both decorate and hem the edge of blankets. It is also used in embroidery and – when the stitches are sewn close together – it is used to edge buttonholes.

1 Imagine two parallel stitch lines roughly ¼in (6mm) apart. Bring the thread through to the front of the work on the top line. Insert the needle ¼in (6mm) further along on the bottom line and through to the front again parallel to where it was inserted, at the same time keeping the working thread under the needle point.

2 Pull the thread through and to the right to form an 'L' shape.

3 Reinsert the needle ¼in (6mm) further along in the bottom line and through to the front again parallel to where it was inserted before, keeping the working thread under the needle. Pull the needle and thread through and to the right again. Continue thus to make a line of blanket stitch.

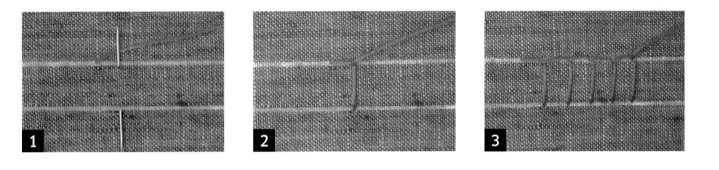

## COUCHING STITCH

This stitch is used for creating lines and outlines, straight or curved.

1 With one thread, make a long straight stitch – 2in (5cm) long or more. Bring a second thread out to the front of the fabric to one side of and up very close to the long stitch, just ⅛in (3mm) from its beginning. Make a small stitch by inserting the needle on the other side of the long stitch, thus anchoring the original in place.

2 Bring the needle out to the front again about ⅜in (1cm) further along the long stitch.

3 Continue making small stitches along its length, anchoring it to the fabric. Rather than completing the first long stitch, leave the thread free, anchoring it as you lay it along a drawn line.

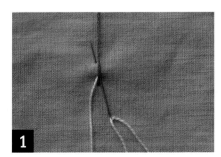

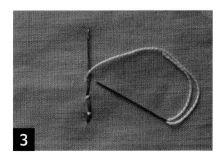

## FRENCH KNOTS

1 Bring the thread out to the front of the fabric. Hold the thread down where it emerges with the thumb of your other hand and wrap the thread three times around the needle's point with your sewing hand.

2 Pull the needle, sliding the 'wraps' of thread down the needle, holding them in place with your thumbnail, and then sliding them down to the fabric surface to create a small knot.

3 Insert the needle back through, close to where the thread first emerged (not in the exact same place or it will simply pull back through). Pull the needle through to the back, leaving the knot on the surface.

4 Bring the needle through to the front again in position for the next knot.

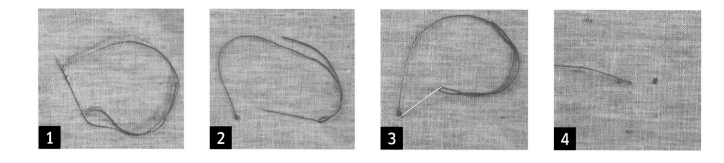

## SATIN STITCH

This stitch fills in areas with embroidery thread to give an effect of solid colour. Before stitching, draw guide lines outlining the area to be filled.

1 Draw the thread through to the front of the fabric at a point on one of the guide lines. Re-insert the needle at a point on the opposite guide line so that it crosses the area to be filled. Bring the needle back out through at a point very close to the place from which it first emerged.

2 Repeat step 1, inserting the needle back down through the fabric very close to the position from the previous step.

3 Continue this action, traversing the gap between the two stitch lines. At the same time, keep the stitches close enough to cover the surface of the fabric.

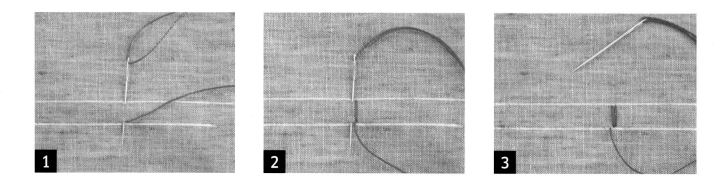

## SEWING ON BUTTONS

With your thread doubled, tie a knot at the end. Pull the needle through to the front of the fabric. Sew the button on securely through the holes, then pull the needle through so that the thread lies between the button and the fabric. Wind the thread around the stitches under the button twice. Insert the needle through to the back of the fabric and finish off with a couple of small, tight stitches (see page 26).

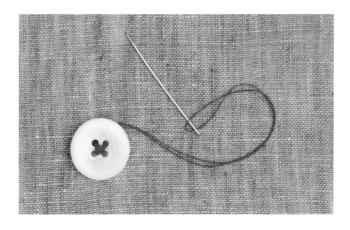

## BUTTONHOLES

Use this method to ensure your buttonholes are a perfect fit for the buttons you have chosen.

1 Using your chosen button as a size guide, mark the position for your button on the fabric – the diameter of your button dictates the length of your buttonhole. For horizontal buttonholes, the position of the button should be near the end closest to the opening. For vertical buttonholes, it should be central. Use small, sharp scissors to cut along the length of the buttonhole.

2 Using sewing thread, make a line of small running stitches around your cut buttonhole – this helps to reduce fraying and holds layers of fabric together if you are working through several thicknesses.

3 Starting at one end of the buttonhole, make very close blanket stitches (see page 17) all around the opening, about ⅛in (3mm) long.

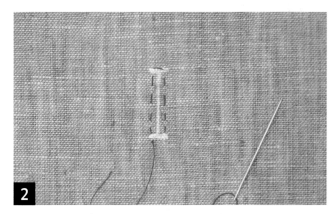

## Tip

*A zipper foot and buttonhole foot on a sewing machine can be very useful extras.*

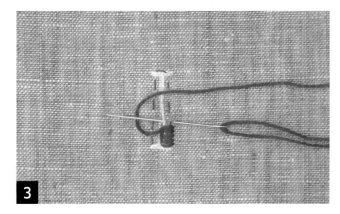

## BUTTON LOOPS

These little hand-made button loops are very satisfying to make and add delicacy to a project.

1 Sew the button on. Use pins to mark the loop's position. Take the folded edge of fabric where the button loop is to go and push the threaded needle up through this folded edge at the point of the left-hand pin, leaving the knotted end within the fold. Push the needle back in again at the point of the right-hand pin, and out again by the left-hand pin. Pull the needle to leave a loop of thread wide enough to go over the button. Repeat stitching through at the two marker pins until the loop has four strands.

2 Remove the pins. Starting at the right-hand side, sew small blanket stitches, encasing the loops of thread you have made. Insert your needle through the loop of four strands so that its tip protrudes beyond the loop. Wrap your thread around the tip of the needle before pulling the needle all the way through to complete one stitch. Draw the thread tightly after each stitch to pull them close together and create a tight cord by wrapping all the loop strands together. Repeat until you reach the left-hand side. Fasten off securely with a few small, tight stitches.

3 Your button should fit neatly into the loop.

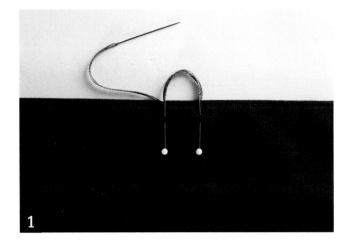

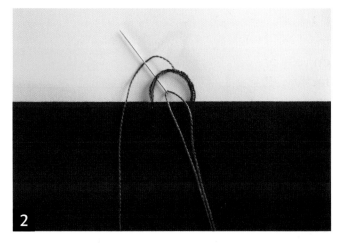

# Tip
*Consider playing around with the colours of the loop as well as the thread used to stitch on the button.*

# MACHINE STITCHES

This book doesn't use fancy sewing machine stitching – the basics of straight stitching, zigzag stitching and reverse stitching are all that's needed for the projects in this book.

## USING A SEWING MACHINE

Set up the machine where there is plenty of light and you can sit comfortably. Before sewing, make sure that the machine is threaded correctly and that the threads from the needle and bobbin are placed away from you, towards the back of the machine. Turn the wheel towards you so that the needle is in the work, preventing a tangle of threads when starting. Taking it slowly will ensure control of the machine and problems with the tension or tangling threads will be less likely.

It's always a good idea to keep any scraps of the fabric you are working with to test out your machine stitch size and tension before starting on your project. If there is a speed restriction facility, it's well worth using this to improve control and accuracy when sewing curves or topstitching. It's important to regularly service the sewing machine and keep it covered when not in use. Always refer to the instruction booklet for information on changing stitches, reversing, making buttonholes etc.

## STRAIGHT STITCH

This stitch is used for all flat seams, hems and topstitching. You can alter the length of straight stitch – when at its longest it can be used for gathering or tacking.

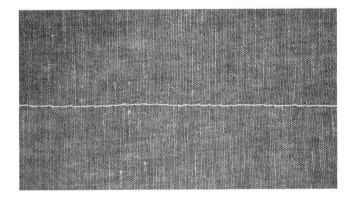

## TOPSTITCH

This is a line of straight machine stitching worked on the right side of the fabric, parallel to seams and edges. Topstitch is used as both a decorative and a functional stitch.

## ZIGZAG STITCH

Used along raw edges to help reduce fraying, zigzag stitch can also be used to strengthen pressure or stress points. It can be used decoratively and for making buttonholes too. For different effects, alter the length of the stitches and how close together they are. When changing from straight stitch to zigzag, or vice versa, without breaking the stitching, always adjust the stitch with the foot down (to hold the fabric in position) and the needle up.

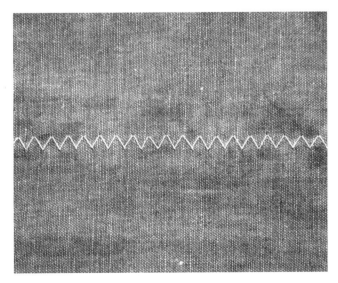

## FLAT SEAMS

Place the two pieces of fabric together, right sides facing and raw edges aligned. Pin or tack the fabric together. Machine stitch along the sewing line, ³/₈in (1cm) from and parallel to the raw edges of the fabrics. Finish the beginning and end of the line of stitching either by hand or by reverse stitching.

## FRENCH SEAMS

This is an efficient way to prevent the raw edges of a seam from fraying. The seam completely encases the raw edges, leaving a neat finish, which is ideal for reversible items or those which get a lot of wear.

1 Place the two pieces of fabric to be joined wrong sides together. Pin or tack before stitching a straight seam along this edge. Trim the seam to ¼in (6mm).

2 Turn the work wrong side out. Tweak and tease the seam with your fingers to make it as neat and sharp as possible. Press the seam and pin or tack along it before stitching a ³/₈in (1cm) seam along it.

3 The raw edges will now be completely encased within the seam.

4 Give the seam a final press to one side with a hot iron.

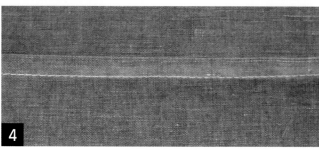

## BOX CORNERS

These corners give body to a bag or cushion and can create a very professional-looking finish.

1 Place two pieces of fabric right sides together. Align the raw edges and pin or tack them together. Using a straight stitch, sew the side and bottom seams. Pivot at the corners by leaving the needle down, raising the foot and turning the fabric 90 degrees.

2 Press the seams open. With the sewn fabric still right sides together, match the side seam with the bottom seam to create a point at one of the corners. Pin to hold them together. It is very important to exactly match the seams; this will make the finished corner look smart.

3 Mark the stitch line of the box corner with a pen or tailor's chalk. Sew across the drawn stitch line several times, reverse stitching at the beginning and end for extra strength. Cut the triangular point of the corner off, leaving a $^3/_8$in (1cm) seam allowance.

4 Turn the work right side out and press neatly. Repeat this process with the other corner.

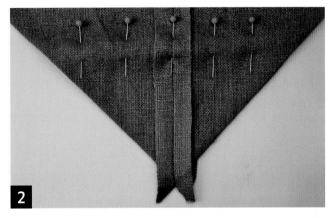

## Tip

*Some projects feature box corners with standard seams, others have French seams (see page opposite). Follow the instructions given within the project.*

## REVERSE STITCHING

This is used to reinforce or strengthen a line of stitching, particularly where pressure or stress will occur, at the edges of a turning gap, for example. Reverse stitching can also be used as an alternative and quick way to start and end stitching without having to finish off thread ends by hand (see page 26).

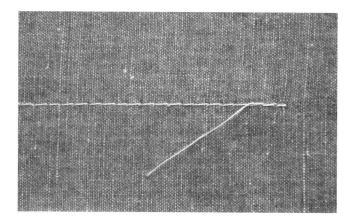

## BINDING STRAIGHT EDGES

Use tape, bias binding or strips of fabric to bind straight raw edges of fabric. As long as the edges are straight and there are mitres at the corners, you do not need to use strips of fabric cut on the bias; shop-bought binding is very easy to use and saves time.

1 Cut the binding to the measurement of the outer edge of your work, plus at least 1in (2.5cm) for joining. Place it on the work right sides together and so that one edge aligns with the raw fabric edge. Pin or tack in position then machine stitch slowly and carefully along the binding fold crease.

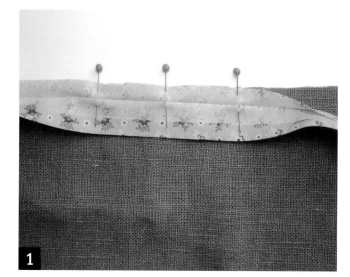

2 Turn your work over. Fold the binding down to meet the stitch line and encase the raw edges. Sew by hand with hem stitch (see page 16).

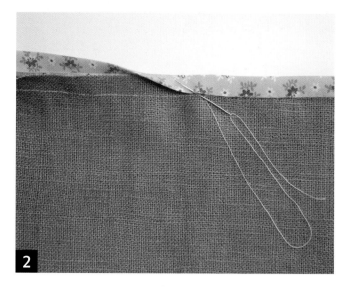

## Tip

*If binding all the way around a piece of work, join it by folding the end under by 3/8in (1cm), overlapping the beginning of the binding and stitching along this fold.*

## BINDING CURVED EDGES

Curved edges require binding with fabric cut on the bias to avoid excessive puckering. The easiest way to do this is to use pre-made bias binding.

1 Open the binding out. Place it on the work right sides together and position the upper fold in the binding along the stitch line. Take time to encourage the binding to follow the curve in the fabric smoothly. Pin or tack in place and machine stitch slowly and carefully along the fold crease.

2 Turn your work over. Fold the binding down to meet the stitch line and encase the raw edges. Sew by hand with hem stitch (see page 16).

3 Turn your work back over again and give it a good press with a hot iron.

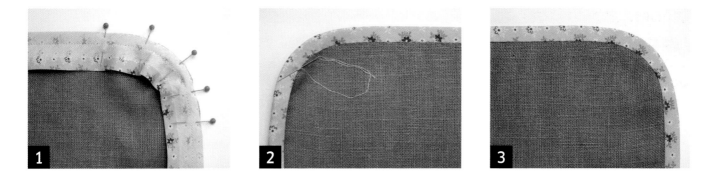

## TURNING GAPS

Usually hidden inside bags, turning gaps are great for producing a really smart finish to projects. They make seemingly invisible joins between outer fabrics and their linings.

1 When sewing the lining of a bag, leave a gap of about 4in (10cm) or more in the line of stitching along one edge. To avoid tearing the seam when you pull the work right side out through it, be sure to reverse stitch as you stop sewing at either side of the gap.

2 Press open the seam where the turning gap is positioned. Turn your work right side out by pulling it through the turning gap. Tweak and tease all the seams and corners to make them sharp and neat, and press with a hot iron. Fold in the raw edges around the gap and pin. Close the gap by hand with overstitch (see page 16).

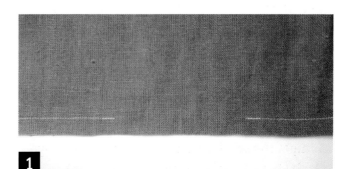

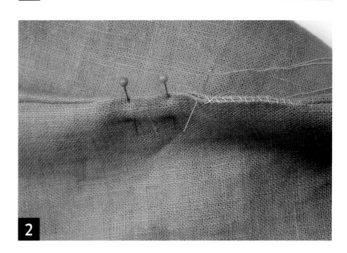

# FINISHING TECHNIQUES

### FINISHING OFF THREADS

When hand stitching, finish off thread ends by threading them onto a sewing needle and either making a couple of small, tight stitches before cutting the thread off, or by 'losing' it into a French seam (see page 22) or hem.

If you have a machine with a reverse mode, simply follow the manual instructions. You could also turn your work 180 degrees and stitch back over the last few stitches: with the needle down through the work, raise the foot, turn the work 180 degrees, lower the foot and make a few stitches. Finish by cutting the tail ends close to the fabric's surface.

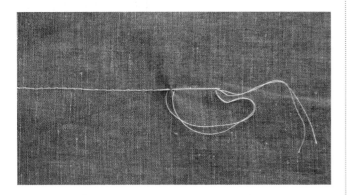

### JOINING TRIMS

If adding trims to a seam, first tack them on to the right side of one piece of fabric accurately before laying the second piece right side down on top of it. To join the two raw ends of trim, fold them at 90 degrees away from the seam line and over the raw edge of the fabric so that the ends are 'lost' within the seam allowance.

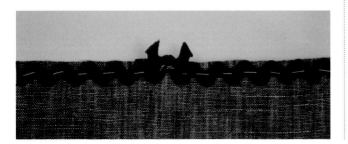

### JOINING PIPING

This can be a bit fiddly, but take it slowly and join the fabric and piping cord before tacking it down onto the seam you are stitching it to.

1 Cover the piping with a strip of bias binding using a piping foot. The length of covered piping needs to be at least 1in (2.5cm) longer than you require. Leave both ends of it open by about 2in (5cm). Cut the two ends of the binding at 45 degrees along the grain of the fabric if it isn't already at this angle. Trim the ends so that each one is ³⁄₈in (1cm) longer than the required length, thus leaving enough binding to stitch a ³⁄₈in (1cm) seam. Place the two binding ends right sides together, and align their short raw edges. Stitch a ³⁄₈in (1cm) seam along this edge and press it open with a hot iron.

2 Trim the two piping cord ends so that they lie flush against each other. Fold the binding down on itself to cover and encase the cord. Tack along the binding snug up to the cord to complete the neat join.

# OTHER TECHNIQUES

## CLIPPING CORNERS AND CURVES

Corners should be cut across at an angle so that they are sharp when the work is turned right side out (A). On curved seams, cut 'V' shapes into the seam allowance close to the stitch line (B). This will make the seam smooth when the work is turned right side out. Snip very carefully with small, sharp scissors to avoid cutting through the seam line by mistake.

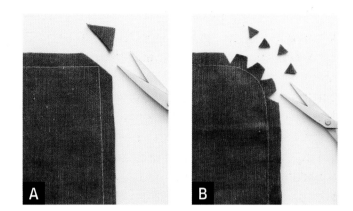

## HANGING LOOP

This is a narrow tube of fabric or bias binding to hang your work to a hook or door handle. Take a piece of fabric 1½in (4cm) wide (unless otherwise stated), and by the required length. Fold each long edge in by ⅜in (1cm) to meet in the centre and press with a hot iron. Fold again so that the two long folded edges meet, and pin or tack. Topstitch ⅛in (3mm) in from both long edges (see page 21).

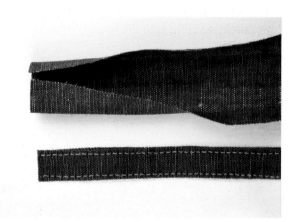

## FIXING EYELETS AND PUNCHING HOLES

Eyelets most often come with a little fixing kit – all you need is a hammer and a solid surface to work on when following the kit's instructions. Alternatively, buy a sturdy pair of eyelet-fixing pliers if you might use eyelets regularly (A).

Holes can be punched in fabric using pliers or with punches and a hammer – if using the latter method, always work on a solid surface and use a disc of hard plastic or solid wood beneath the fabric to protect the work surface (B).

# DECORATIONS

# HANGING HEARTS

These simple, white linen hanging decorations are sweetly scented with winter spices and decorated with tiny silver bells and blanket stitching. Hang them on your tree, along your mantle shelf or in a window. Templates are also supplied for stars and doves.

Find the templates on page 138

You will need
(makes one heart)
6 x 12in (15 x 30cm) of white linen
Hollowfibre stuffing
Winter spices such as star anise, cloves, peppercorns, cardamom pods or cinnamon
Tiny silver bells
Tracing paper or baking parchment
Paper-cutting scissors
Pencil
Sewing machine
Thread to match fabric
Sewing needle
Embroidery needle
Assorted contrasting cotton embroidery threads
White cotton yarn
Pins
Dress-making scissors
Small, sharp scissors
Air-erasable pen
Iron

NOTE: One fat quarter makes four hearts, five birds or four stars.

1 Use the heart template on page 138 to cut out two pieces of white linen. With right sides together, align the fabric edges and pin or tack all the way round, remembering to leave a turning gap as indicated on the template. Sew a ³⁄₈in (1cm) seam around the edge, reverse stitching at either side of the turning gap (see page 24).

2 Following the instructions for clipping corners and curves (see page 27), snip off the seam allowance at the bottom of the heart, clip into the indent at the top and cut 'V'-shaped notches around the two curves, taking great care not to cut through the stitch line. Turn the heart right sides out through the turning gap.

3 Tweak and tease the seams with your fingers to make them sharp and neat and press with a hot iron. Stuff the heart through the turning gap with stuffing and spices – push stuffing in first, spices into the centre, and then more stuffing so that the spices are cushioned by it.

4 Fold the raw edges in at the turning gap and close it by hand using overstitch (see page 16).

5 Using embroidery thread, hand sew around the edge of the heart using an even blanket stitch (see page 17).

6 Using sewing thread, stitch a small bell to the bottom tip of the heart.

7 Create a hanging loop with a length of white cotton yarn or thick embroidery thread using an embroidery needle (see page 27).

## Tip

*Make further designs yourself, such as a tree, a little house or an angel.*

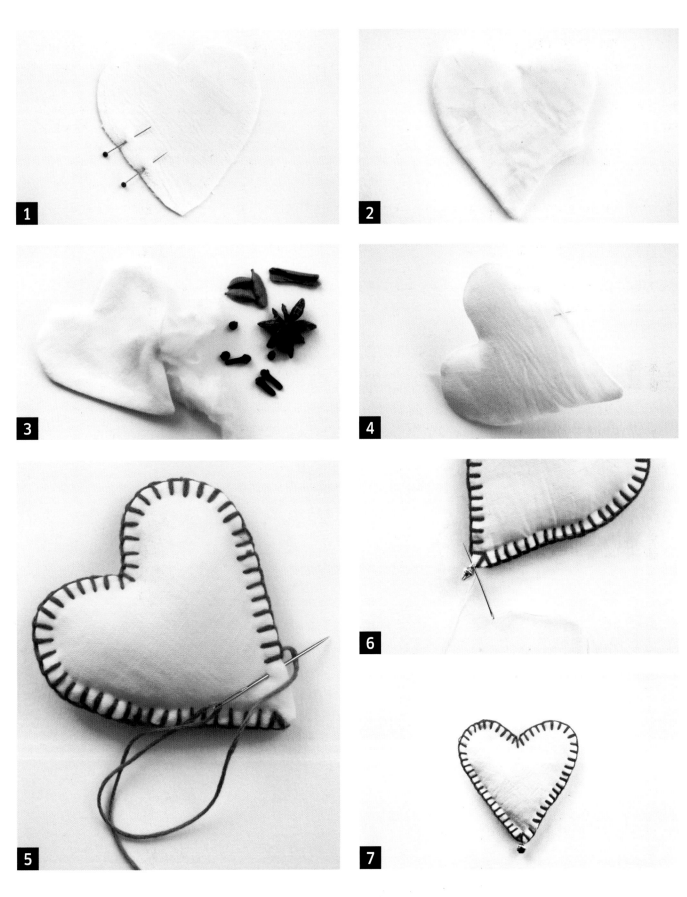

# SNOWFLAKE GARLAND

These simple and quick-to-make graphic snowflakes could hang along a shelf, on your Christmas tree or above a doorway. You could also use them individually as hanging decorations, or to garnish a gift as a little bonus present in itself.

Find the template on page 138

You will need
(for each snowflake)
4 x 8in (10 x 20cm) of dark blue fabric
White cotton embroidery thread
Yarn, string, piping cord or trim to hang snowflakes
Tracing paper or baking parchment
Paper-cutting scissors
Embroidery needle
Measuring tape or ruler
Sewing machine
White thread
Sewing needle
Pins
Pencil
Small, sharp scissors
White pen or tailor's chalk
Iron

NOTE: One fat quarter makes ten snowflakes.

1 Use the template on page 138 to cut out the fabric circles. Place the two pieces of fabric right sides together. Align the edges, then pin or tack all the way round, marking a turning gap as indicated on the template. Sew a ³/₈in (1cm) hem around the edge, reverse stitching at each side of the turning gap (see page 24).

2 Use small, sharp scissors to cut notches in the seam allowance (see page 27), apart from along the turning gap.

3 Turn your work right sides out, through the turning gap. Tease and tweak the seam with your fingers to make it as crisp and neat as possible, folding the raw edges in around the gap, before pressing with a hot iron. Close the gap by hand with overstitch (see page 16).

4 Fold the fabric into quarters and pinch the point of the folds to determine the centre of the circle. Open the fabric out again and mark the crossed creases at the centre with a white pen or tailor's chalk. Use the notches on the template to divide the circumference of your fabric circle into six. Use measuring tape or a ruler and a white pen or tailor's chalk to join these marks, creating guide lines for your stitching.

5 Set the machine to a fairly close zigzag stitch, about ³/₁₆in (5mm) wide, and sew along the drawn lines. Finish off the thread ends by hand.

6 Now stitch six 'V's around the outer edge at the end of each line – again, using zigzag stitch and following the template – to complete the snowflake motif. Finish off the thread ends (see page 26).

7 Make a small button loop at the edge of your fabric (see page 20). Use the circumference of a pencil to ensure your loops are the same size for each snowflake. Wrap the embroidery thread around the pencil and re-insert the needle, pulling it to fit around the pencil. Gently remove the pencil before sewing blanket stitches (see page 17) around the loop of thread.

8 Make more snowflakes and thread them onto the trim or string you are using – tie small knots around the button loops if they slip around too much, to keep them in place.

## Tip

*You could also make some contrasting snowflakes in pale fabrics with dark blue stitching.*

# TREE BUNTING

Jolly up the Christmas tree with little flag bunting made from myriad small print fabrics in various tones of red, pink and orange. Make as long a string of these ribbon-like flags as you wish. You can make the flags smaller, though this will be fiddly – be careful when pressing them so you don't burn your fingertips.

Find the template on page 139

You will need
(for each flag)
2 small pieces of fabric, at least 4½ x 3¼in (11.25 x 8cm) each
1in (2.5cm)-wide tape or bias binding to your required length
Tracing paper or baking parchment
2 x ⅛in (3mm) eyelets and fixing kit (optional)
Sewing machine
Thread to match fabric
Tacking thread
Sewing needle
Pins
Sharp scissors
Pencil
Paper-cutting scissors
Air-erasable pen or tailor's chalk
Iron

NOTE: One fat quarter will make at least 13 flags, but there's no need to use the same fabric on both sides.

1 Use the template on page 139 to cut out two pieces of fabric for each flag. Place these pieces right sides together and align all their raw edges. Pin or tack together before straight stitching a ¼in (6mm) seam along one long side, the chevron (upside-down 'V') bottom edge, and the second long side. Start and finish with reverse stitching for extra strength (see page 24).

2 Trim the two points of the chevron with sharp scissors, then snip into its inner point, taking great care not to cut through the stitch line by mistake.

3 Turn the work right sides out. Prod the two points of the chevron from inside with a blunt tool such as a knitting needle, and then pick carefully at them with a pin from the outside to make them neat and sharp.

4 Tease and manipulate the straight seams to make them as neat as possible before pressing the work firmly with a hot iron – be careful not to scorch your fingers when pressing small pieces of work. The apex of the chevron may look rather puckered. This will improve with pressing – if not, make the snip inside slightly longer, but beware: if you go too far you will end up with a hole here!

5 Repeat steps 1–4 to make all the flags. Take the tape (or bias binding) and fold it in half all along its length. At 8in (20cm) from one end, slot one of the flags snugly into the tape so that its raw edges fit very tightly into the pressed crease. Fold the tape back down over the flag and pin or tack in position.

6 Insert the remaining flags, leaving 1in (2.5cm) gaps between each until they are all in position. Fold in both short raw ends of the tape and pin or tack in place. Topstitch ⅛in (3mm) from the edge of the tape (see page 21) through all layers of fabric from one end to the other, reverse stitching at the beginning and end for strength.

7 If you like, fix a ⅛in (3mm) eyelet at either end of the tape (see page 27). Your bunting can then be used at any other celebration, easily hung from hooks or thumb tacks.

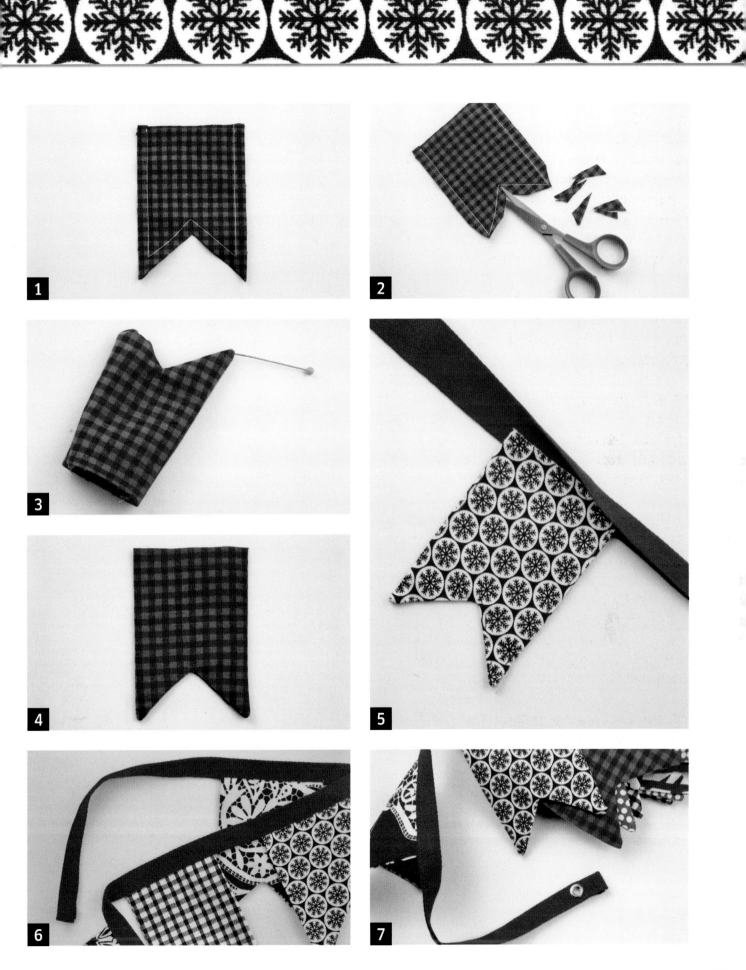

# PINWHEEL DECORATIONS

Add a little extra colour to your seasonal styling with these quick-to-make, no-sew pinwheels. These striking hanging decorations, with a nod towards classic Christmas poinsettia flowers, look wonderful on a tree or in a window.

You will need
(for one pinwheel)
2 x 20in (5 x 51cm) piece of each of two fabrics
2 x 20in (5 x 51cm) piece of iron-on adhesive
1¾in (4.5cm) pompom maker
Large, sharp sewing needle
Cotton embroidery thread
Yarn
Fabric glue or double-sided tape
Small crochet hook (optional)
Large bulldog clip or a couple of clothes pegs
Sharp scissors
Iron

NOTE: One fat quarter makes five pinwheels.

## Tip
*Make a dozen or more pinwheels and attach them to an evergreen wreath to adorn your front door during the festive season.*

1 Use a hot iron and the iron-on adhesive to fuse the two pieces of fabric, wrong sides together.

2 Fold the fabric strip into a concertina, each fold roughly ½in (12mm) wide. If using double-sided tape rather than fabric glue to fix your pinwheel, stick a strip of it along the edge of one short end of the fabric.

3 Thread your needle with embroidery cotton and push it through the folds of fabric 3/16in (5mm) from one end.

4 Draw your needle all the way through and tie a firm knot with the two thread ends to draw the fabric into a pinwheel.

5 Fix the two short ends of the fabric together to complete the pinwheel by either peeling off the double-sided tape's backing paper or applying fabric glue. Hold the two ends in place using a large bulldog clip or a couple of clothes pegs.

6 Use sharp scissors to snip points at the ends of the folds on the outer edge all the way around the pinwheel.

7 Make two half pompoms – follow the manufacturer's instructions, but wrap the yarn around one half of the pompom maker only each time. Use 20in (51cm) of yarn to tie the pompom, keeping the long ends to attach your half pompoms later.

8 Snip at the pompoms to give them a smooth surface all over.

9 Take one of the pompoms and use a needle or a small crochet hook to pull one yarn end through the centre of the pinwheel to the other side. Do the same with the other pompom so that you now have one yarn end from each half pompom on each side of the pinwheel.

10 Tie a tight knot with the two yarn ends on both sides of the pinwheel and trim the ends to the same length as the pompom so they simply become part of them.

11 Use your needle to make a loop at the edge of the pinwheel with 8in (20cm) of embroidery cotton, tying the two ends together.

1

2

3

4

5

6

7

8

9

10

11

# FAIRY-LIGHT SHADES

Give your fairy lights a fantastic festive makeover with these cute little shades made from the smallest of fabric scraps. These little cones of fabric add pretty, colourful interest even when the lights are switched off.

**Find the template on page 139**

You will need
(for each shade)
1 x 3in (7.5cm) diameter circle of fabric and fusible interfacing
Tracing paper or baking parchment
Pencil
Paper-cutting scissors
Pinking shears
Sewing machine
Thread to match fabric
Pins
Sharp scissors
Air-erasable pen or tailor's chalk
Iron

NOTE: One fat quarter will make 25 light shades.

## Tip
*Only use LED lights for this project, and remember to turn fairy lights off when you leave the room.*

1 Use the template on page 139 to cut out the fabric and interfacing. Take the circle of interfacing and, using a hot iron, fuse it to the wrong side of the fabric circle. Remember to double check that the interfacing lies glue-side down before pressing.

2 Set your machine's stitch to a short and fairly close zigzag stitch before topstitching ³/16in (5mm) in from the edge of the circle (see page 21), as indicated on the template. This line of stitching will help to reduce fraying. Sew a small line of topstitching near the centre of the circle, again, following the template.

3 Use pinking shears to cut a decorative zigzag edge for the shade.

4 Fold your circle, right sides together, in half along the dotted line marked on the template. Using a straight stitch, machine sew along the line indicated on the template. Starting at the fold, stitch to the outer raw edge and, with the needle still down in the fabric, raise the foot and turn your fabric 180 degrees before sewing back down to the fold again, sewing over the stitches again. Trim the excess fabric very close to the stitch line with sharp scissors. You should now have a small fabric cone.

5 Use the tip of your sharp scissors to snip three times from the pointed centre of the cone of fabric up to the inner zigzag stitch line – take care to snip up to, but not into, these stitches.

6 Repeat steps 1–5 to create as many shades as required. Push a conical shade over each small light bulb on your string of lights to complete the project.

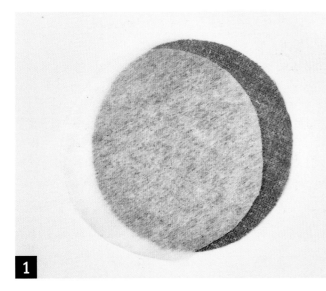

1

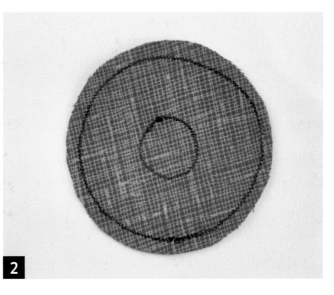

2

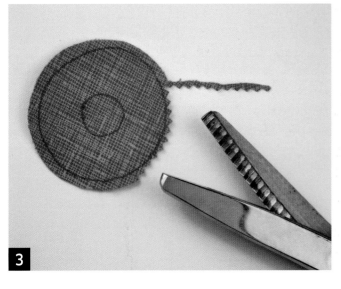

3

4

5

6

# ACCESSORIES

# WINTER TREE

This simple conical tree is made Christmassy with a snowy dusting of embroidery. It has a weighted base to prevent toppling and can be used on its own or grouped with more trees and snow-laden houses (see page 56) to create a nostalgic winter world.

Find the templates on page 140

You will need
10 x 7in (25 x 18cm) of fabric
7 x 7in (18 x 18cm) of fusible interfacing
3 x 3in (7.5 x 7.5cm) of fusible stabilizer
Some dried pulses
Hollowfibre stuffing
Small sheet (A5) of thin card
Tracing paper or baking parchment
Pencil
Paper-cutting scissors
Embroidery needle
White cotton embroidery thread
Sewing machine
Thread to match fabric
Sewing needle
Tacking thread
Pins
Sharp scissors
Air-erasable pen or tailor's chalk
Iron

NOTE: One fat quarter makes six trees.

**1** Use the template on page 140 to cut out the pieces for the tree body. Fuse the interfacing to the wrong side of the fabric with a hot iron. The picture shows fabric cut out for two trees.

**2** Use white cotton embroidery thread and an embroidery needle to decorate the fabric pieces with French knots (see page 18) and stars (the stars are done by crossing three long stitches over each other). Do this randomly, or follow the pattern indicated on the template on page 140.

**3** Fold the fabric, right sides together, so that the two straight sides align. Pin or tack along this edge then machine sew a ³⁄₈in (1cm) seam, reverse stitching at either end (see page 24) and leaving a turning gap as indicated on the template. Snip the seam allowance at the point at the top, taking great care not to snip the stitches.

**4** Use a hot iron to press the seam open – be careful of your fingertips!

**5** Cut a circle of fabric and a circle of fusible stabilizer using the tree base template on page 140. Use a hot iron to fuse the stabilizer to the centre of the wrong side of the fabric.

**6** Pin and then tack the base to the bottom of the embroidered piece, right sides together. Take your time to minimize the risk of puckering when you stitch the seam.

**7** Machine stitch a ³⁄₈in (1cm) seam around the base, taking it very slowly to ensure as wrinkle-free a join as possible. Remove the tacking.

**8** Turn your work right sides out through the turning gap and use a pin to pick at the top and make the tip as sharp and neat as you can.

**9** Make a funnel from a piece of paper or card secured by a pin. Slot it into the turning gap and pour or spoon in dried pulses to fill about 1in (2.5cm) of the base of the tree.

**10** Now stuff the rest of the tree with hollowfibre stuffing.

**11** Tuck the raw edges in at the turning gap and close it by hand using overstitch (see page 16).

## Tip

*Add a couple of deer and some cotton-wool snow to complete the Christmas scene.*

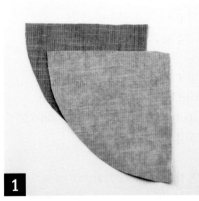

1

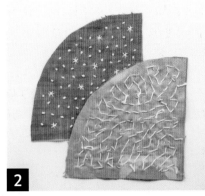

2

3

4

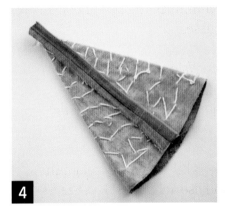

5

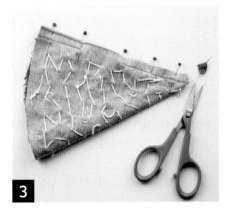

6

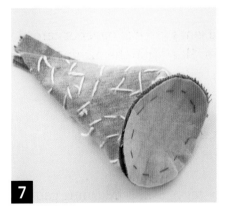

7

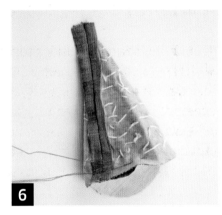

8

9

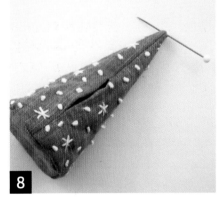

10

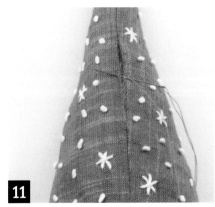

11

# WINTER HOUSE

This sweet little winter chalet-style house with its snow-laden roof can adorn any table or create a winter scene on a mantel shelf. Place on a bed of cotton wool or quilt wadding, nestled amongst embroidered winter trees, to complete the look.

Find the templates on page 141

You will need

11 x 7in (28 x 18cm) of fabric and fusible interfacing
    for the walls and base
7 x 4¾in (18 x 12cm) of white linen and stabilizer for the roof
4 x 1¾in (10 x 4.5cm) of fabric and iron-on adhesive
    for the doors and windows
Some dried pulses such as split peas or lentils
Hollowfibre stuffing – several large handfuls
Tracing paper or baking parchment
Pencil
Paper-cutting scissors
Sewing machine
Thread to match fabric
Sewing needle
Pins
Sharp scissors
Air-erasable pen or tailor's chalk
Iron

NOTE: One fat quarter will make the base and walls of three houses – use stash fabrics for the windows and roofs.

1 Use the templates on page 141 to cut out the fabric for the house main piece and roof pieces. Cut out the fusible interfacing pieces and, using a hot iron, fix them to the wrong side of the house piece. Follow the template for the positioning – there should be gaps of 1/8in (3mm) between each piece of interfacing (indicated by red lines on the template) and a 3/8in (1cm) seam allowance around the edges. Fix the two pieces of stabilizer to one of the roof pieces, leaving a 1/8in (3mm) gap between them and a 3/8in (1cm) seam allowance around the edges.

2 Fuse the iron-on adhesive to the back of your doors and windows fabric. Cut strips of fabric 3/8in (1cm) wide, then cut six pieces 5/8in (1.5cm) long from the strip for windows and two pieces 1in (2.5cm) long for the doors. Peel off the backing paper and use a hot iron to fix the doors and windows to the right side of the house fabric piece in the positions indicated on the template.

3 Use a small and close zigzag stitch to stitch the windows and doors to the house. Leave the bottom of the doors unstitched.

4 For the house wall, with right sides together, fold the fabric so that point A meets point B. Align the raw edges and pin or tack before sewing a 3/8in (1cm) seam, stitching just beyond the edge of the interfacing, stopping at point A/B and reverse stitching at either end (see page 24).

5 Now fold your work so that point C meets point D. Pin or tack before stitching a 3/8in (1cm) seam along this edge, just outside the edge of the interfacing. Start at point A/B and finish at point C/D, reverse stitching at either end.

6 Finally, fold the fabric so that point E meets point C/D and point F meets point G. This creates an 'L'-shaped seam. Pin along it before stitching from C/D to E, reverse stitching at either end. Remove your work from the machine and reposition it to stitch from C/D/E to F/G, again reverse stitching at either end.

7 Turn the house the right way out, using a pin to pick at the corners to make them as sharp and neat as possible – no need to clip the corners before this, as the excess fabric helps to fill the corners. Fold the raw edge all around the top of the house in by 3/8in (1cm) and tack it in position.

8 Now make the snowy roof. Place two pieces of white linen right sides together and align the raw edges. Pin or tack together before stitching a 3/8in (1cm) seam around, just beyond the edge of the stabilizer. Remember to leave a turning gap as on the template. Reverse stitch at either end.

9 Clip the roof corners diagonally (see page 27) and then turn right sides out through the turning gap. Pick at the four corners with a pin and tweak and tease the seams to make them nice and sharp. Fold the raw edges in at the turning gap. Press with a hot iron before closing the gap by hand using overstitch (see page 16).

10 Fold the roof piece in half along the space between the two pieces of stabilizer inside it. Join the roof to the top edge of the walls by hand, using overstitch, leaving one side open for filling. The roof edges should overhang the top of the walls by about 1/4in (6mm).

11 Spoon dried pulses in through the gap left between the roof and walls until it reaches about 1in (2.5cm) from the base.

12 Stuff the rest of the house with hollowfibre stuffing and finally close the gap between the roof and walls by hand with overstitch.

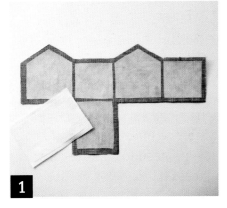

1

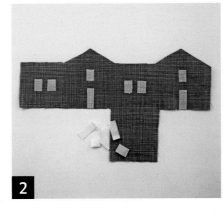

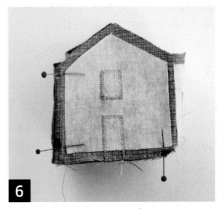

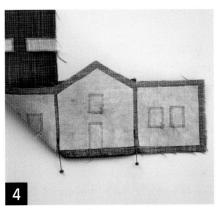

4

5

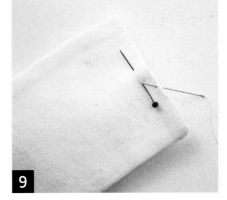

7

8

10

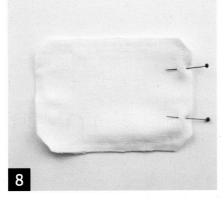

11

12

# BONBON DISH

This is a really pretty little reversible bowl for sweet treats – a very quick project that can be made larger or smaller simply by adjusting the templates. You could make several and fill them with baubles or pinecones to decorate different rooms in your house.

Find the templates on page 142

You will need
1 fat quarter of dark fabric
1 fat quarter of light fabric
18 x 18in (46 x 46cm) of stabilizer
24x 24in (61 x 61cm) of iron-on adhesive
Sewing machine
Thread to match fabric
Tracing paper or baking parchment
Paper-cutting scissors
Pencil
Pins
Sharp scissors
Air-erasable pen or tailor's chalk
Iron

NOTE: Two fat quarters makes one bowl measuring approximately 10in (25cm) diameter, 3in (7.5cm) high.

1 Use the templates on page 142 to cut six of template A and one of template B from the light fabric, dark fabric and stabilizer. Cut twelve of template A and two of template B from the iron-on adhesive. Use a hot iron and iron-on adhesive to fuse the stabilizer to the wrong side of their corresponding pieces of light fabric. Now use the iron-on adhesive and a hot iron to adhere the wrong side of the pieces of dark fabric to the stabilizer side of the light fabric pieces. Make sure everything is stable by topstitching just 1/16in (2mm) in from the edges of all seven pieces (see page 21). You should end up with stabilizer sandwiched between the two pieces of patterned fabric.

2 Take one A piece and the B piece and place them dark side up. Butt the straight, narrow edge of A to one side of the hexagon piece (B). Use a wide and close zigzag stitch – 1/4in (6mm) wide is best – and stitch along this join. Work with the machine's foot centred along the join so that the stitching extends to the same distance onto each of the two pieces. Reverse stitch at either end for extra strength (see page 24).

3 Repeat step 2 with the remaining five A pieces.

4 Flip your work so the light fabric is facing up. Now start joining the six side seams. Start stitching from one corner of the base hexagon and working out in the same zigzag stitch forwards to the outer edge of the dish. Reverse stitch at the beginning and end for extra strength.

5 When all six side seams are completed, use very sharp scissors to even out any irregular joins along the top edge.

6 Finally, zigzag stitch all the way around the outside edge of the dish. Test a little bit of stitching first to see if the zigzags are close enough to cover the top edge, the raw ends of the fabric and the white of the stabilizer – you may have to make the stitch closer to achieve this.

## Tip

*Make one dish using numerous fabrics and thread colours to create a patchwork effect.*

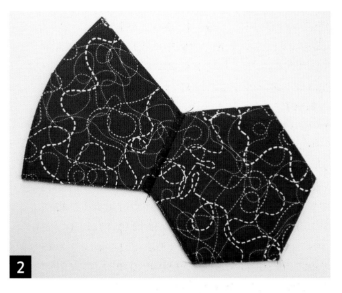

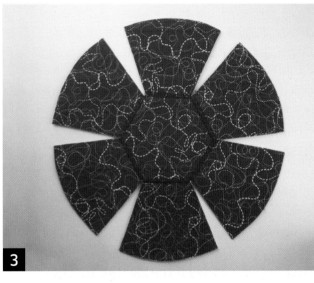

# CARD RIBBON

Christmas cards are traditionally displayed pinned to a length of ribbon. In this more sophisticated and enduring version, narrow strips of fabric are bordered by tiny white pompoms and a variety of leftover buttons are stitched over paperclips. Once pushed into the clips, your cards will look as if they've been stitched on with a button.

Find the templates on page 142

You will need
2 strips of fabric measuring 1½ x 43in (4 x 109cm)
90in (2.3m) of tiny pompom (or alternative) trim
6 x buttons
6 x paperclips
Tracing paper or baking parchment
Pencil
Paper-cutting scissors
Sewing machine
Thread to match fabric
Tacking thread in two colours
Buttonhole jig for sewing machine (optional)
Sewing needle
Pins
Sharp scissors
Air-erasable pen or tailor's chalk
Iron
Nail or thumbtack for hanging

NOTE: One fat quarter makes three ribbons, and each strip will hold six cards. You will need to join two strips of fabric 1½ x 21¾in (4 x 55.5cm) with a ⅜in (1cm) seam (pressed open) to achieve the lengths specified.

1 Use the template on page 142 to cut curves on either end of both fabric pieces. Place one strip right side facing up. Tack the long length of trim around it with the edge to be exposed and facing in towards the fabric's middle, and with the other edge aligned with the fabric's raw edge. Overlap the ends by 3/8in (1cm) and twist them 45 degrees. Position the tacking carefully on the trim, then machine stitch the trim down for 4in (10cm) along one straight edge, following this tacking line. This will be the turning gap. Place the other piece of fabric on top, right side facing down. Using a different coloured thread, tack all the way around, leaving a 3in (7.5cm) gap along one straight edge, centred over the 4in (10cm) stitched-down trim.

2 Mark the turning gap clearly with pins before machine sewing around the edge of the work, following the tack line. Start at one side of the turning gap and finish at the other, reverse stitching at both ends for extra strength (see page 24). Try to use a seam of just 3/16in (5mm) so there is no need to clip the curves.

3 Turn your work right sides facing out through the turning gap – use a blunt tool such as a knitting needle to prod one end out.

4 Do the same with the other end. Once the whole thing is turned out, tweak and tease the edges with your fingers to make them sharp and give it a good press with a hot iron.

5 Fold in the raw edges at the turning gap and pin it before closing it by hand using overstitch (see page 16).

6 Mark and stitch a buttonhole ½in (12mm) from one end of the ribbon by hand or by machine (see page 19).

7 Sew on the first button (see page 19), 3in (7.5cm) below the buttonhole. Trap a paperclip underneath the button, with the button stitching straddling and anchoring the paperclip to the ribbon. Now sew on five further buttons, each one 6in (15cm) apart.

8 Use the top buttonhole to hang the ribbon by a nail or thumbtack. Fold the top over and push the first button through the buttonhole if you are hanging it from a rod or pole.

# TEA-LIGHT HOLDER

This sweet fabric holder will cover a jam jar and a tea light. The fabric softens and hides its contents, producing an atmospheric, warm glow with spots of clear light shining as star-like specks through little embroidered holes.

Find the template on page 142

You will need
(to fit over a jar measuring 9¼in (23.5cm) in circumference and 4in (10cm) in height)
10½ x 4¾in (26.5 x 12cm) of outer fabric and white linen
11in (28cm) length of ¾in (2cm)-wide bias binding
Tracing paper or baking parchment
Pencil
Paper-cutting scissors
Sewing machine
Thread to match fabric
Tacking thread
Embroidery needle
Cotton embroidery thread
Sewing needle
Pins
Sharp scissors
Air-erasable pen or tailor's chalk
⅛in (3mm) hole punch pliers (or a hammer, a punch and block to cushion it)
Jam jar
Tea light
Iron

NOTE: One fat quarter of outer fabric and one fat quarter of white linen make four tea-light holders.

CAUTION: Never leave lit candles unattended.

1 Place the two pieces of fabric right sides together and pin or tack along one long edge. Stitch a ³⁄₈in (1cm) seam along this edge, remove the tacking and press open.

2 Fold your work in half, right sides facing together and aligning the two short ends. Pin or tack along this long edge, matching up the seam ends from step 1, before stitching a ³⁄₈in (1cm) seam along this edge. Remove the tacking and press this new seam open.

3 Now fold along the original seam to create a cylinder of fabric – the white linen lining tucked inside the outer fabric, wrong sides together. Trim along the raw edge to make the two raw fabric edges even.

4 Take the piece of binding and trim it to the exact circumference of the fabric cylinder plus ¾in (2cm). Open out the binding and place the two ends right sides facing together, aligning their raw edges to make a circle. Pin or tack and then stitch a ³⁄₈in (1cm) seam along this edge. Remove the tacking and press this short seam open before re-folding the binding and giving the whole thing a press.

5 Tack the binding around the raw edge of the fabric cylinder, pushing this edge snugly into the centre fold of the binding. Tack carefully around, being sure to catch the binding's edge with your stitches on both the outside and the inside of the work.

6 Topstitch (see page 21) along the binding to secure it to the fabric and make a neat bottom edge for the holder. Remove the tacking. Use a hole punch to make the embroidery holes. If not using pliers, make sure you protect the opposite side of the work from the punch by placing a small plastic disc between them – these are often supplied with punches and eyelet kits. Position these holes randomly, or trace and then cut out the template on page 142, using it as a guide.

7 Thread the embroidery needle with cotton embroidery thread and neaten the raw edge of the punched holes with a circle of blanket stitches (see page 17).

8 As you finish working each hole, run the needle back through a couple of stitches before using sharp scissors to snip the tail end close to the surface of the fabric. Slip the work over a jam jar and light a small tea light within it.

## Tip

*Make holders in different sizes depending on the height and circumference of your jam jar.*

1

2

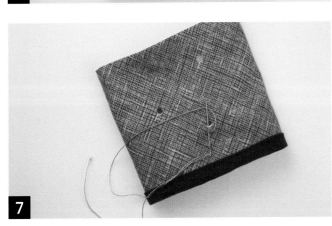

3

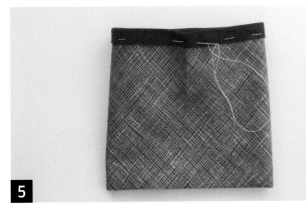

4

5

6

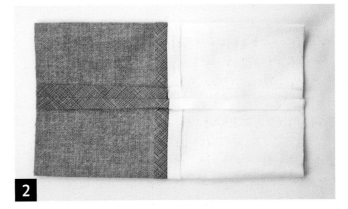

7

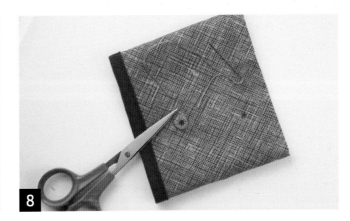

8

# THE DINING
# TABLE

# MISTLETOE NAPKINS

These festive, cocktail-sized napkins are embellished with an embroidered mistletoe motif and are perfect for handing out with Christmas drinks and nibbles. Linen washes beautifully and has the benefit of improving with wear.

Find the template on page 140

You will need
(makes one napkin)
6½ x 6½in (16.5 x 16.5cm) of red linen
Embroidery needle and cotton embroidery threads in white and various shades of green and blue
3 x small assorted white buttons
Tracing paper or baking parchment
Pencil
Paper-cutting scissors
Small crochet hook (optional)
Sewing machine
Tacking thread
Thread to match fabric
Sewing needle
Pins
Sharp scissors
Air-erasable pen or tailor's chalk
Iron

NOTE: One fat quarter will make nine napkins.

1 Right side down, fold the four edges of the fabric square in by ³/₈in (1cm) all the way around and tack in position.

2 Fold each edge over again by another ³/₈in (1cm) and tack down to form a hem around all edges.

3 Machine stitch the hem, just ¹/₁₆in (2mm) from the edge. Press with a hot iron.

4 Using the template on page 140, trace the mistletoe motif onto one corner of the right side of the napkin. Using satin stitch (see page 18), fill in the leaves with green cotton embroidery thread.

5 Sew the stems of the leaves with couching stitch (see page 17). Tidy the thread ends at the back with a small crochet hook or an embroidery needle, losing the ends in the back of the stitching.

6 With the white embroidery cotton doubled, sew on one of the buttons (see page 19).

7 Stitch on the remaining two buttons to finish the design.

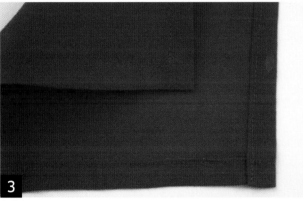

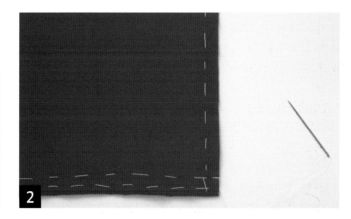

# PLACEMENTS

This is a luxurious way to mark your seating arrangements for a special meal. The designs are a cross between enamelled French house number plates and iced cookies. They are ideal for using up fabric scraps and very short lengths of trim.

Find the templates on page 143

You will need
(for each placement)
5 x 12in (12.5 x 30cm) of backing fabric
5 x 6in (12.5 x 15cm) of white linen
4 x 4in (10 x 10cm) of stabilizer
3 x 2in (7.5 x 5cm) of wadding
9½in (24cm)-length of trim
Cotton embroidery thread
Tracing paper or baking parchment
Pencil
Paper-cutting scissors
Embroidery needle
Sewing machine
Thread to match fabric
Sewing needles of different sizes
Pins
Sharp scissors
Air-erasable pen or tailor's chalk
Iron

NOTE: One fat quarter of backing fabric and half a fat quarter of white linen will make at least four placements, or use stash fabrics to the measurements indicated.

1 Use the templates on page 143 to cut two ovals in the backing fabric. Place right sides together and align the raw edges. Pin or tack before sewing a ³⁄₈in (1cm) seam all the way around, remembering to leave a turning gap as indicated on the template. Reverse stitch at the beginning and end of the seam to give it extra strength (see page 24).

2 Use sharp scissors to trim the seam allowance to ¹⁄₈in (3mm), apart from at the turning gap.

3 Cut a piece of stabilizer using the template and roll it up so that you can manoeuvre it through the turning gap. Insert your finger to unroll it so that the stabilizer fits snugly inside the fabric oval.

4 When you are happy with the fit, fold the raw edges in at the turning gap, press the work with a hot iron and close it by hand using overstitch (see page 16).

5 Cut an oval of white linen using the template. Trace your chosen letter on to the centre of the linen – do this up against a window or use a light box if you have one. Use the embroidery thread and needle to fill the letter using satin stitch (see page 18).

6 With sewing thread doubled and a smaller needle, sew a line of running stitch (see page 16) ¹⁄₄in (6mm) in from the raw edge of the linen. Do not finish off the thread and leave the needle attached.

7 Cut a piece of wadding and a piece of stabilizer using the smallest oval template. Place the embroidered linen right side down, lay the wadding on the centre of it and the stabilizer on top of that. Now draw the thread gently to gather the edge of the linen around the wadding and stabilizer. Tweak and tease the fabric so that the seam allowance is even all the way around. Keeping the tension of the gathers, make a few firm stitches on top of each other to hold the whole thing in position.

8 Take the piece of trim and start stitching it to the back of the padded and embroidered panel using overstitch – fold the lead raw edge over towards the middle of the panel and turn the work over regularly as you stitch to ensure that you are happy with its positioning.

9 Once you have completed sewing on the trim, fold the finishing end down towards the centre of the panel as you did with the lead end, and cut off any excess. For a speedy finish, you can glue the embroidered panel onto the centre of the back panel, but it's nicer to stitch it down, sewing through all layers, using overstitch and catching the very edge of the white linen as you work around it.

# Tip

*Simple, embroidered initials are quick enough to stitch, but if you have the time and patience, why not embroider full names?*

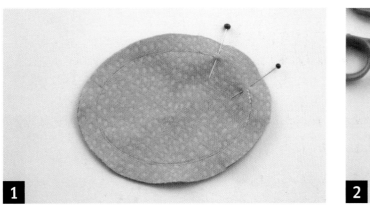

**1**
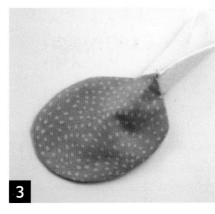

**3**
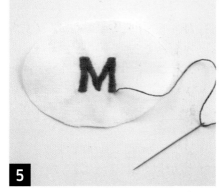

**4**

**5**
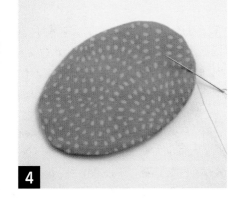

**6**

**7**

**8**

**9**

# CUTLERY POCKETS

This is a neat and useful way to smarten up any table setting. Each one has a pocket for cutlery and a separate one for a napkin. Use the rivet hole on the front to tie on a bow or some jingling bells – or you can add a gift tag with a name on it as a placement.

Find the templates on page 143

You will need
(for each pocket)
½ fat quarter of fabric for the back panel
½ fat quarter of fabric in a contrast fabric for the pockets
7 x 10in (18 x 25cm) fusible interfacing
1 x ⅛in (3mm) eyelet and eyelet gun or fixing kit (optional)
Tracing paper or baking parchment
Pencil
Paper-cutting scissors
Sewing machine
Thread to match fabric
Pins
Sharp scissors
Air-erasable pen or tailor's chalk
Iron

NOTE: You can make the whole project from the same fabric – one fat quarter will make one cutlery pocket.

1 Use the templates on page 143 to cut out the angled pocket pieces, the back panel and the front pocket from the fabric and the interfacing. Fix the interfacing to the wrong side of one of the angled pocket pieces and the front pocket piece, following the position guides.

2 Place the two angled pocket pieces right sides together and align all the raw edges. Pin or tack along the angled edge and machine stitch a $^3/_8$in (1cm) seam along it.

3 Press the angled seam to one side, then fold one side down to meet the other, wrong sides together, and press with a hot iron before top stitching $^1/_8$in (3mm) from the folded edge (see page 21). Fold the front pocket piece in half, wrong sides together along the edge of the interfacing, and press with a hot iron before top stitching $^1/_8$in (3mm) from the folded edge.

4 Lay one back panel piece right side up and position the angled pocket piece on top of it. Align the sides and bottom and pin or tack in place. Stitch a straight seam $^3/_4$in (2cm) from the bottom edge.

5 Turn your work over and trim the seam allowance to $^3/_{16}$in (5mm).

6 Turn the work over again. Now take the front pocket piece and place it on top of the work.

7 Position the front pocket so that it overhangs the bottom edge by $^1/_2$in (12mm) and align the raw side edges. The right-hand top corner of the pocket should lay about $^3/_8$in (1cm) above the same corner of the angled pocket. Turn your work over and top stitch along the two sides to hold all three layers in position.

8 Lay the second back piece right side down on top of the work, covering the two pockets, and align the raw edges. Pin or tack in position.

9 Machine stitch a $^3/_8$in (1cm) seam around the sides and top edges, leaving the bottom edge open. Clip the top two corners diagonally with sharp scissors (see page 27).

10 Push your hand into the work through the open bottom and between the two pocket pieces. Pull it right sides out – you should end up with the angled pocket on one side of your work and the front pocket on the other. With the side with the angled pocket facing up, press the bottom raw edges of fabric before pinning or tacking them. Stitch a $^3/_8$in (1cm) seam along this edge.

11 Clip the two bottom corners diagonally before turning your work right sides out – do this by slipping your hand into the front pocket and flipping it over the bottom of the work to the other side. Pick at the corners with a pin to make them sharp before pressing the work with a hot iron.

12 Fix a $^1/_8$in (3mm) eyelet to the centre of the front pocket (see page 27), $^3/_8$in (1cm) from the top edge.

## Tip

*You needn't make the pockets all the same colours – this is a good opportunity to use up all sorts of fabric scraps.*

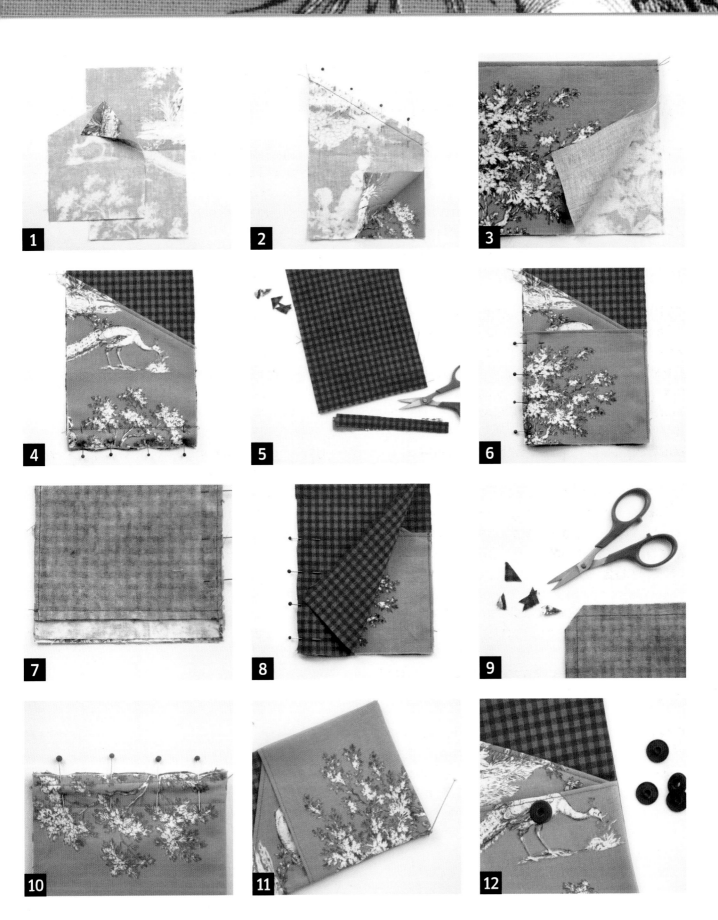

# NAPKIN RINGS

This fantastic little project will use up scraps of fabric and assorted buttons. Roll up a napkin, measure the circumference around it, and adjust the measurements to ensure the ring will fit snugly – this one has a 5in (12.5cm) circumference once buttoned up.

Find the templates on page 144

You will need
(for each napkin ring)
14¾ x 2⅜in (37.5 x 6cm) white linen
4 scraps of assorted fabrics for leaves measuring
    4 x 2½in (10 x 6.5cm) each
4 x 2½in (10 x 6.5cm) iron-on adhesive
14 x 1½in (35.5 x 4cm) fusible interfacing
Sewing thread in various colours and to match buttons
2–3 red or pink small buttons, approximately ⅜in (1cm) diameter
1 x white button, approximately ⅜in (1cm) diameter
Tracing paper or baking parchment
Pencil
Paper-cutting scissors
Sewing machine
Buttonhole jig for your machine (optional)
Sewing needle
Pins
Sharp scissors
Air-erasable pen or tailor's chalk
Iron

NOTE: One fat quarter of white linen and a handful of patterned stash fabrics will make eight napkin rings.

1 Use the templates on page 144 to cut out the linen and interfacing pieces. Fuse the interfacing to one side of the linen, leaving a 3/8in (1cm) seam allowance all the way around. Turn the fabric over. Set the machine to a 3/16in (5mm) wide and close zigzag stitch. Using your chosen colour of thread, stitch a thick stem for the holly, following the template motif.

2 Fold the fabric in half, right sides together, so that the two short ends align. Pin or tack before stitching 3/8in (1cm) seams around the three raw edges – remember to leave a turning gap as indicated on the template. Reverse stitch at either side for extra strength (see page 24).

3 Clip the four corners diagonally with sharp scissors (see page 27), taking care not to snip the stitching. Turn the work right sides out through the turning gap.

4 Tease and tweak the seams, tucking in the raw edges at the turning gap. Pick the corners with a pin to make them nice and sharp before pressing the whole thing with a hot iron and top stitching 1/16in (2mm) in from the edge all the way around (see page 21).

5 Stitch a buttonhole to accommodate the white button vertically and 3/8in (1cm) from one short end. Do this by hand (see page 19), or by machine using a buttonhole jig.

6 Sew on the white button at the other short end (see page 19), centrally and 3/8in (1cm) in from the edge.

7 For the leaves, fuse a piece of iron-on adhesive to the wrong side of one of the green pieces of fabric using an iron. When cool, peel off the backing paper and, aligning the edges, lay another piece of fabric wrong side down on top of it. Cut out a holly leaf template from page 144, pin it in place and draw around it on the green 'sandwiched' fabric. With the paper template still in place, follow the stitch guide to top stitch an outline on the leaf with straight stitching – take it slowly as you will be stitching quite tight curves and corners.

8 Remove the paper template to machine stitch veins onto the leaf in the same way. Use sharp scissors to cut out the leaf 1/8in (3mm) outside the stitched outline.

9 Decide which side is the leaf front before folding it in half, front sides together. Pin and then top stitch from the bottom of the fold in the leaf to halfway up, just 1/16in (2mm) in from the fold. Leave the needle down in the fabric, raise the foot and turn your work 180 degrees before lowering the foot and stitching back down to the bottom again.

10 Repeat steps 7–9 to make a second leaf. Move the two leaves on the napkin ring until you're happy with their positions. Pin or tack them down and stitch the bottom half of the stem to the linen by machine.

11 Using matching thread, stitch on two or three red or pink buttons to finish off the napkin ring.

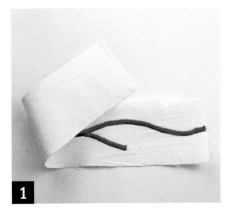

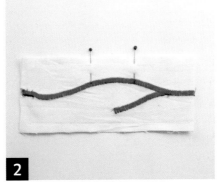

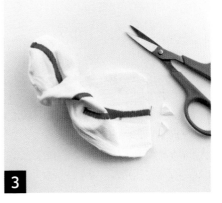

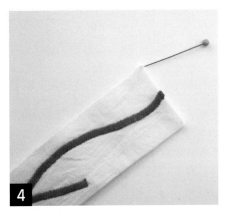

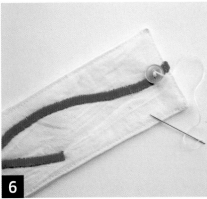

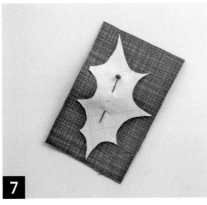

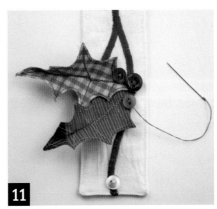

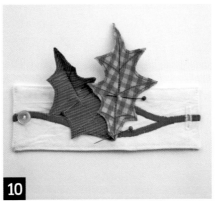

# THE WINTER FIRESIDE

# MANTEL EDGING

Use this scalloped gingham trim to edge your mantel shelf. Assorted buttons stitched between the scallops not only add little jewels of interest, but can also be used to hang baubles and little heirloom decorations, piling on luxury and glitz.

Find the template on page 144

You will need
Fabric and fusible interfacing: the length of the front
    and sides of the mantel x 6½in (16.5cm)
Assorted red, green and white buttons of various sizes
    (twice the number of scallops, minus two)
Tracing paper or baking parchment
Pencil
Paper-cutting scissors
Sewing machine
Thread to match fabric
Sewing needle
Measuring tape or ruler
Pins
Sharp scissors
Air-erasable pen or tailor's chalk
Iron
Adhesive putty or sticky pads

NOTE: One fat quarter of fabric will be enough for edging measuring up to 60 (150cm) long – use ³⁄₈in (1cm) seams to join 6½in (16.5cm) strips together to achieve the length you require.

1 Use a hot iron to fuse the interfacing to the wrong side of the fabric.

2 Fold the fabric in half with the two long edges and right sides together. Align all the edges and press the long fold with an iron. Use the template on page 144 to mark the fabric for stitching. Find the fabric's centre and draw the scallops along its length, laying the straight edge along the fabric fold. Work from the centre point, marking the pattern to either end so that the scallops are distributed evenly across your work.

3 Starting and finishing with reverse stitch (see page 24), sew along the marked line from one end to the other. Work slowly to achieve nice smooth curves. You may even want to reverse stitch as you enter and leave the sharp angled point between each scallop to reinforce these areas. Stitch a 3/16in (5mm) seam along one end, but leave the other end open for turning later. Trim the seam allowance to 3/16in (5mm) then snip into each of the sharp angles between the scallops, taking great care not to cut into the stitch line.

4 Turn the work right sides out through the end that has been left unstitched. Tweak and tease the curved seam with your fingers to make it as sharp as possible before pressing firmly with a hot iron. Do not be too concerned if there is slight puckering in between the scallops as you will be able to disguise some of this with the buttons.

## Tip

*Make this edging in plain white linen and trim with pompoms or rickrack for a crisp, clean look.*

5 Move around the buttons until you are happy with the order they will be in. You can use single buttons of various shapes and sizes, or place a small button on top of a larger one to add interest. Once you are happy with their distribution, stitch them firmly between the curves (see page 19).

6 Fold the raw edges in at the end with the turning gap and pin or tack it before closing it by hand with overstitch (see page 16). Attach the edging to the mantel shelf using adhesive putty or sticky pads.

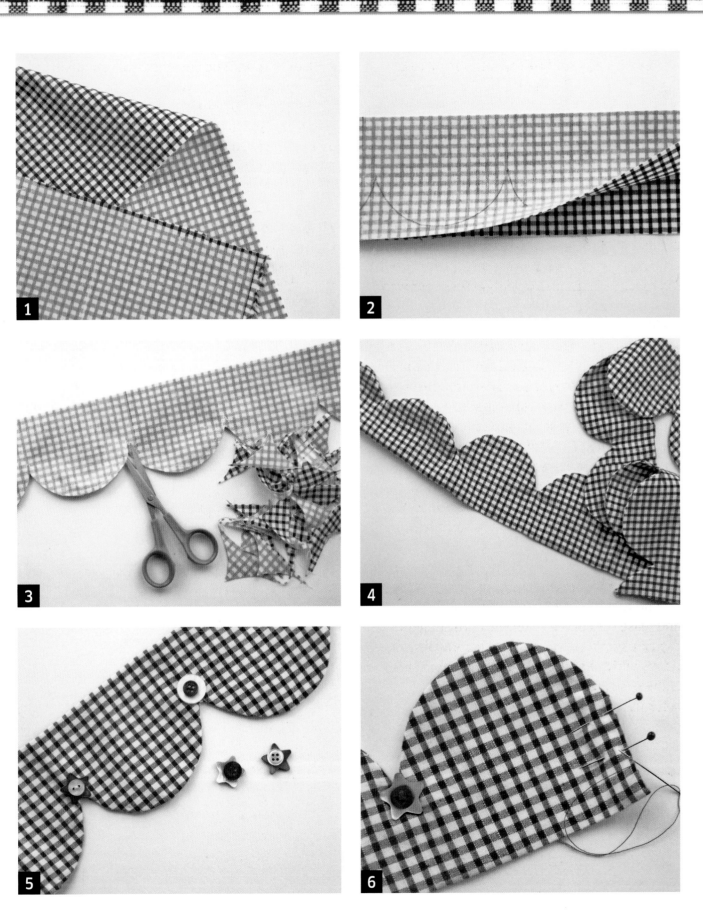

# KINDLING BAG

Make this sturdy bag to store kindling close to hand. Its bold, graphic fabric and the angle of the handles give it a strong look, and the wide mouth makes it easy to fill. Add handmade plaited paper firelighters to make a great present for someone.

Find the templates on page 144

You will need
2 fat quarters of outer fabric: you will need a 36¼ x 10in (92 x 25.5cm) rectangle and a 12in (30cm) diameter circle
2 fat quarters of lining fabric: you will need a 36¼ x 10in (92 x 25.5cm) rectangle and a 12in (30cm) diameter circle
35½ x 9¼in (90 x 23.5cm) rectangle and 11¼in (28.5cm) diameter circle of fusible wadding
22 x 1in (56 x 2.5cm) of webbing for the handles
Tracing paper or baking parchment
Pencil
Paper-cutting scissors
Protractor or ruler with angles marked
Sewing machine
Thread to match fabric
Sewing needle
Tacking thread
Pins
Sharp scissors
Air-erasable pen or tailor's chalk
Iron

NOTE: Join the fat quarters together with a ³/8in (1cm) seam to achieve the measurements required or use two continuous fat quarters.

## Tip
*Make several bags in different patterns to be used for storage, or even to hold presents under the tree.*

1 Take the rectangle of outer fabric and, right sides together, fold it so the two short edges align. Pin or tack along this edge before machine stitching a ³∕8in (1cm) seam. Press the seam open with a hot iron.

2 Use a hot iron to fix the fusible wadding to the wrong side of the rectangle of lining fabric, centring it to leave a seam allowance of ³∕8in (1cm) all the way around. Right sides together, fold it so the two short edges align, as you did with the outer fabric. Pin or tack along this edge before machine stitching a ³∕8in (1cm) seam. Press the seam open with a hot iron.

3 Use the template on page 144 to cut out the circles for the base. Topstitch ¹∕4in (6mm) in from the outside edge of both the outer fabric and lining (see page 21) to help them retain their shape while you're working. When joining a curved edge to a straight edge (in the next step), it also helps to reduce puckering and tucks. Use a hot iron to fuse the wadding to the wrong side of the outer fabric just inside the topstitching line, leaving a ³∕8in (1cm) seam allowance all the way around.

4 Take the two pieces of outer fabric and, with right sides together, and the piece from step 1 still inside out, use pins to join the base circle to the sides. First fold your circle into eighths and mark these points with pins around its outer edge. Divide the bottom raw edge of the sides in the same way. Pin together each of the eight marked points on the base circle to each pin on the sides. Working methodically around the basket, align the raw edges between pins, adding further pins to hold the two layers of fabric in place. Now stitch a ³∕8in (1cm) seam so the line falls just outside the edge of the base wadding. Repeat this with the two pieces of lining fabric.

5 Press the circular seam of the outer fabric towards the bag's sides and pin or tack it in place. Turning your work right sides out, topstitch ¹∕4in (6mm) from the circular seam and on the bag's side piece, sewing through both layers of the seam allowance as well as you do so. Repeat with the lining.

6 With the outer fabric still right sides out, fold the top edge in by ³∕8in (1cm) and tack in place. With the lining inside out, fold the top edge down over the wadding by ³∕4in (2cm) all the way around – this will give you ³∕8in (1cm) of double thickness of wadding along the top edge. Now place the lining inside the outer fabric bag, wrong sides together. Align the side seams of each piece. Align the top folded edges all the way around and pin.

7 Prepare the handles by cutting the length of webbing in half. Use a protractor to draw two lines ³∕4in (2cm) apart and at a 60-degree angle at each end – refer to the template, and note that the angles at the ends mirror each other. With sharp scissors, trim all ends to 60 degrees on the angled line nearest the end of the webbing.

8 On one side of your work, locate the centre – about 9in (23cm) from the vertical seam – and mark it with a pin. Tuck one end of one of the handles ³∕4in (1cm) between the outer and the inner pieces, 2in (5cm) to one side of the centre marking pin and 2in (5cm) to the other side of the marking pin, and pin in place. Repeat on the other side with the second handle.

9 Working from the outside, topstitch around the bag ¹∕8in (3mm) from the top edge and ³∕8in (1cm) below that stitch line. Reverse stitch over the handles for extra strength (see page 24).

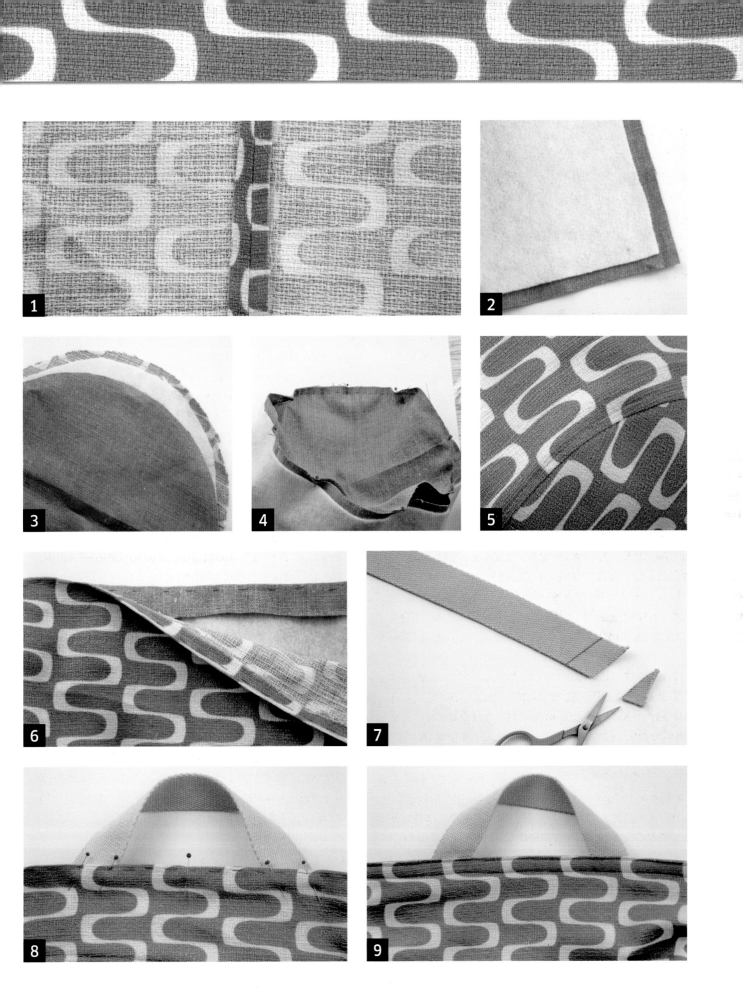

# SPILL HOLDER

Spills or long matches for lighting fires are easily scattered and lost amongst kindling. Store them in this smart, slender holder, made from fabric scraps and fusible stabilizer. Hang the holder by its loop, or tuck it up against the side of your kindling or log basket.

Find the templates on page 145

You will need
½ fat quarter of outer fabric
½ fat quarter of lining fabric
9¾ x 7³/₈in (25 x 19cm) of fusible stabilizer
4¾ x ³/₈in (12 x 1cm)-wide herringbone tape
Tracing paper or baking parchment
Paper-cutting scissors
Pencil
Sewing machine
Thread to match fabric
Sewing needle
Tacking thread
Pins
Sharp scissors
Air-erasable pen or tailor's chalk
Iron

NOTE: You can make two holders from one fat quarter if you use the same material for the outer and lining fabric.

1 Use the template on page 145 to cut out the fabrics. Use an iron to fuse the stabilizer to the wrong side of the outer fabric. Centre it, glue side down, so that it sits with a ³⁄₈in (1cm) seam allowance all the way around before fixing it with the iron.

2 Prepare the hanging loop (see page 27). Take the length of herringbone tape and fold it in half lengthways. Press with a hot iron before stitching along its length by machine ¹⁄₈in (3mm) from the aligned edges.

3 Lay the outer fabric right side up. Pin the folded loop hanging downwards ⁵⁄₈in (1.5cm) in from the top right–hand side of the fabric, with its raw short ends protruding beyond the edge by about ¹⁄₄in (6mm). Now lay the lining fabric right side face down on top of the outer fabric.

4 Align the raw fabric edges and pin or tack along the top edge before stitching a ³⁄₈in (1cm) seam. Press the seam towards the outer fabric and tack it down.

5 Turn your work over and topstitch (see page 21) on the outer fabric, ³⁄₁₆in (5mm) from the seam.

6 Now fold your work in half, right sides together and aligning the two long edges. Pin all the way around, remembering to leave a turning gap as indicated on the template. Stitch a ³⁄₈in (1cm) seam all the way around the raw edges, starting and ending with reverse stitching either side of the gap (see page 24).

7 With your work still inside out, create box corners for the base of the holder, firstly at the outer fabric end. Use the template to determine the position of the box corner seams. Do the same again at the lining end. See also Box Corners, page 23.

8 Turn your work right sides out through the turning gap. Fold in the raw edges at the gap and close it by hand using overstitch (see page 16). Finish by pushing the lining snugly into the outer and giving the whole thing a good press with a hot iron.

## Tip

*You can easily adjust this spill holder's depth to suit your needs. Ideally the spills will protrude a couple of inches at the top, so adjust the length of your holder accordingly, taking into account seam allowances and the box corners at the bottom.*

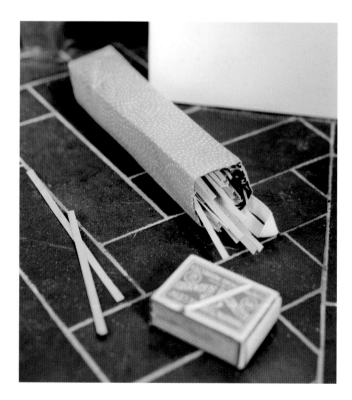

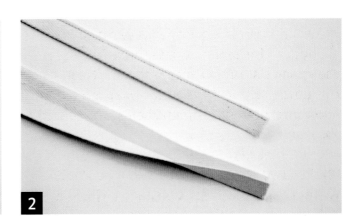

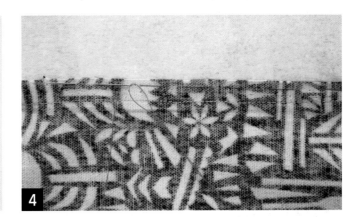

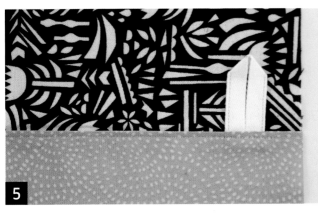

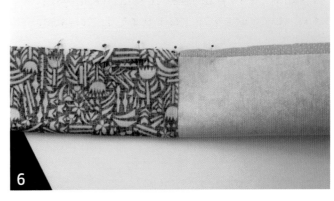

# HEARTH CUSHION

Make a cushion decorated with pompom 'snowballs' to soften your seat on the hearth. This is simply stuffed with a hollowfibre pillow and, if you make the pompoms with washable yarn, you can put the whole thing in the wash if it gets a bit sooty.

You will need
2 fat quarters of grey linen
1½ x 6in (4 x 15cm) of contrasting fabric for the hanging loop
75in (190cm) of bias binding (or make your own from patterned fabric)
75in (190cm) of piping cord
6 x ³⁄₈in (1cm) buttons
Standard rectangular hollowfibre pillow for stuffing
White DK yarn
1¾in (4.5cm) pompom maker
Yarn or darning needle
Sewing machine
Thread to match fabric
Zipper foot
Sewing needle
Pins
Sharp scissors
Air-erasable pen or tailor's chalk
Iron

1 Make the hanging loop. Take the piece of contrasting fabric and fold each long edge in by $^3/8$in (1cm) to meet in the centre and press with a hot iron. Fold again so that the two long folded edges meet and pin or tack. Topstitch $^1/8$in (3mm) in from each long edge (see page 21).

2 Place the piping cord within the bias binding. Using a zipper foot, machine stitch along the folded strip, right up next to the piping to encase it with the patterned fabric. Start and finish your stitching 3in (7.5cm) from either end of the strip.

3 Cut the fat quarters of linen down to 22 x 16in (56 x 40cm) each. Place one piece of linen right side up and pin or tack the covered piping all around it, the raw edges aligning with the raw edge of the linen.

4 At a point $^3/8$in (1cm) from each corner, clip the piping seam allowance diagonally, taking great care not to snip the stitching, so that you can bend it around the corner.

5 Along one short edge of the linen, position the hanging loop. Fold it in half and pin so that the loop hangs towards the middle of the fabric at the centre of the edge, with one raw end lying either side of the piping, protruding slightly beyond the raw edge of the cushion.

6 Join the two piping ends by stitching the ends together to create the required length and trimming the seam to $^3/8$in (1cm) and pressing it open. Cut the ends of the piping so that they butt together. Fold the fabric down to encase the piping ends and pin or tack in place. See also Joining Piping, page 26.

7 Sew along the stitch line of the piping for a 8in (20cm) section of one long edge – this will be the position of the turning gap. Place the second piece of linen right side down on top of the first and pin or tack all the way round, marking the turning gap. Stitch a $^3/8$in (1cm) seam all the way round, reverse stitching at either side of the gap for extra strength (see page 24). Turn the work right side out through the gap. Push the pillow into the cushion cover. Tuck the raw edges in and close the gap by hand using overstitch (see page 16).

8 Using your pompom maker, make six pompoms with the white yarn. Retain the two long yarn ends used to tie them together for attaching the pompoms to the cushion. Thread the yarn ends onto a long yarn or darning needle and feed them from the front through to the back of the cushion at regular intervals (see the position guide on page 145).

9 Turning the cushion over, and with just one tail of yarn in the needle, feed the needle through from the back of the button to the front, then back through to the back again. Do the same with the second tail end through the remaining two buttonholes (if the button has four) or through the same two holes but in the opposite order (if your button has just two).

10 Now tie the two tail ends in a knot to secure the button on this side and the pompom on the other. Pull the ends firmly to create plump cushioning as you tie the knot between the button and the fabric surface.

11 Trim the tail ends with sharp scissors so that they sit behind the button.

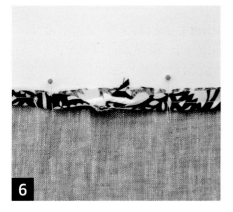

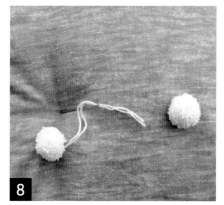

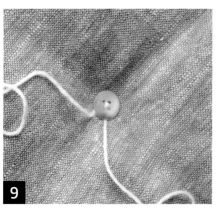

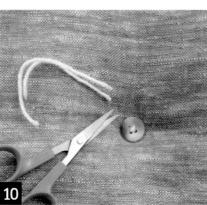

# TRADITIONAL STOCKING

These clean, crisp linen stockings are trimmed with cheerful jingling bells around the cuff, giving a feeling of tradition and nostalgia. If you plan to make several, use different linings for each, or add embroidered initials on the red cuff to personalize them.

Find the templates on pages 148–9

You will need
1 fat quarter of natural linen for outer (B)
1 fat quarter of gingham for lining (C)
½ fat quarter of red linen for cuff (A)
1½ x 7¾in (4 x 19.5cm) fabric for the hanging loop
16in (40.5cm) length of large white rickrack
12 x silver bells, ½in (12mm) diameter
Tracing paper or baking parchment
Pencil
Paper-cutting scissors
Sewing machine
Tacking thread
Thread to match fabric
Sewing needle
Pins
Sharp scissors
Air-erasable pen or tailor's chalk
Iron

1 Use the templates on pages 148-9 to cut out all the fabric pieces. Place the two outer pieces of fabric (B) wrong sides together and align their raw edges. Pin or tack around the two layers of fabric, leaving the straight top edge open. Stitch a 3/8in (1cm) seam all the way around. Clip the curve where the leg curves into the ankle and cut small 'V's at the curve of the heel and toes (see page 27).

2 Place one cuff piece and one lining piece right sides together and align their top edges. Pin or tack in position before stitching a 3/8in (1cm) seam. Press the seam open with a hot iron. Do the same with the other lining and cuff pieces.

3 Make a hanging loop from the small piece of fabric following the instructions on page 27. Now place the two lining and cuff pieces right sides together and align all their raw edges. Start pinning or tacking all the way around, incorporating the loop 1/4in (6mm) below the seam joining the cuff and the lining, as on the template. Make sure the folded end of the loop lies towards the middle of the fabric and the raw short ends protrude just 3/8in (1cm) beyond the raw edge.

4 When you get to the other side, remember to mark a turning gap, as shown on the template. Stitch a 3/8in (1cm) seam around the edge of the stocking lining and cuff, leaving the top of the cuff open. Reverse stitch at either side of the turning gap and over the hanging loop for extra strength (see page 24).

5 Trim the seam allowance to 3/16in (5mm) all the way around, apart from at the gap.

6 Turn your work right sides out and add the rickrack around the top edge of the cuff, tacking along its centre to hold in place. Turn the raw ends up and over the edge of the cuff where you start and finish.

7 Turn the outer stocking right sides out and give it a press. Turn the cuff and lining piece inside out, so the right sides are facing together, and slip the outer piece inside it.

8 Push the outer piece down snugly so that the top raw edges and their seams align. Pin or tack around the top before machine stitching a 3/8in (1cm) seam.

9 Turn your work right sides out through the turning gap.

10 Tuck the raw edges in at the gap and pin the two sides together before closing by hand using overstitch (see page 16).

11 Push the outer linen snugly down inside the lining and cuff piece. Tweak and tease the top seam until it is nice and neat before pressing the stocking cuff. Pin or tack through all layers along the seam joining the cuff to the lining. Topstitch (see page 21) along here 1/8in (3mm) to the cuff side of the seam – you may have to remove the front section of the machine bed to do this, so that you can slip the cuff of the stocking over the remainder of the bed.

12 Turn the work linen sides out and push the lining right down inside. Use a needle with thread doubled to sew little silver bells evenly along the edges of the rickrack.

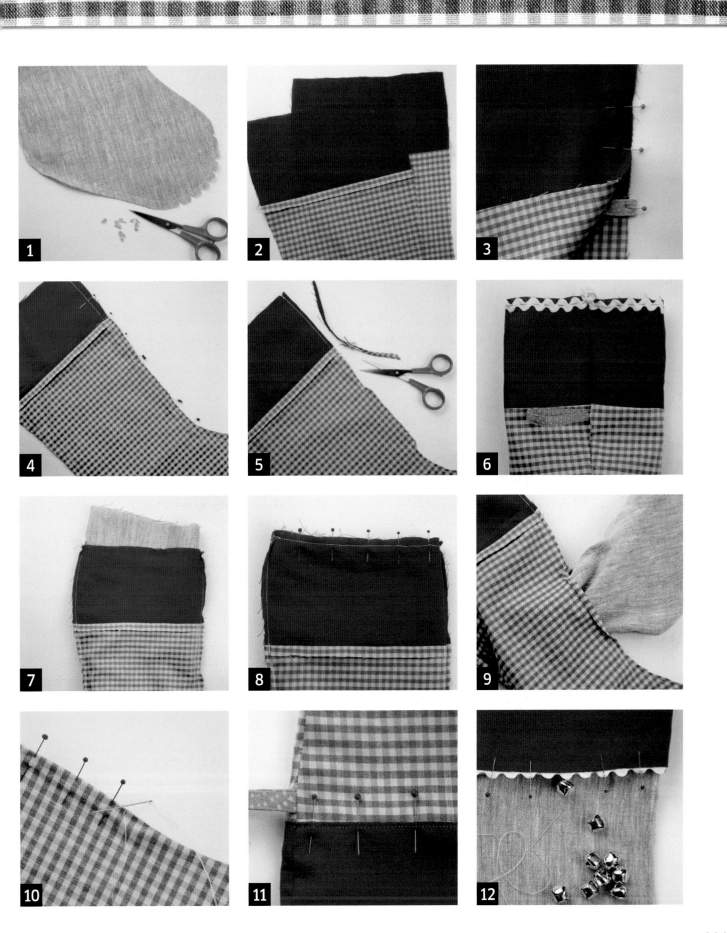

# STRIPED STOCKING

Make a striped stocking using patchwork patterned fabrics trimmed with pompoms to create your own family heirloom. You could even embellish the stocking with embroidery stitches, or use alternative trims and buttons to add extra detail and character.

Find the templates on pages 148-9

You will need
18 strips of 1½ x 8in (4 x 20cm) fabric for stripes
½ fat quarter of cuff lining fabric (D)
½ fat quarter of outer cuff (A), heel and toe fabric
1 fat quarter of lining fabric (C)
1½ x 7¾in (4 x 19.5cm) fabric for the hanging loop
16in (40cm) length of ½in (12mm) diameter pompom trim
Tracing paper or baking parchment
Paper-cutting scissors
Pencil
Sewing machine
Thread to match fabric
Sewing needle
Tacking thread
Pins
Sharp scissors
Air-erasable pen or tailor's chalk
Iron

NOTE: Use fabric scraps from your stash to make the stripes and hanging loop.

1 Use the templates on pages 148-9 to cut out the fabric pieces. Start by piecing the fabrics for the outer of the stocking. Take one of the cuff lining pieces and place it right side up. Take the first stripe strip and lay it along the bottom raw edge of cuff lining, right side down. Pin or tack in position before stitching a $^3/_{16}$in (5mm) seam along this edge.

2 Carry on adding the next three strips in this way, then the outer heel. Press the seams towards the heel piece. Repeat this process with the foot section, starting with the foot heel piece, then the strips, finishing with the toe. Press the seams towards the toe.

3 Lay your 'window' templates E and F over your pieced fabrics, taking time to position the notches before marking and cutting them. Topstitch $^1/_8$in (3mm) in from the edges to make them more stable (see page 21).

4 Lay the two outer pieces right sides together and pin or tack the two heel piece edges. Stitch a $^3/_8$in (1cm) seam along this edge. Press this seam towards the toe.

5 Repeat steps 1–4, but reverse the 'window' templates for the other side of the stocking. Place the two patched pieces right sides together and align the raw edges. Pin or tack all the way around, leaving the top edge open. Stitch a $^3/_8$in (1cm) seam all the way around. Clip the curve where the leg meets the ankle and cut small 'V's at the curve of the heel and toes (see page 27).

6 Join the cuff pieces to the lining pieces, placing right sides together, aligning their top edges. Pin or tack together before stitching a $^3/_8$in (1cm) seam. Press the seams open.

7 Make a hanging loop from the small piece of fabric (see page 27). Place the two lining and cuff pieces right sides together and align their raw edges. Pin or tack all the way around, incorporating the loop $^1/_4$in (6mm) below the seam from step 6, as indicated on the template. Make sure the folded end of the loop lies towards the middle of the fabric and the ends protrude just $^3/_8$in (1cm) beyond the raw edge. Remember to mark a turning gap, as shown on the template.

8 Stitch a $^3/_8$in (1cm) seam, leaving the top of the cuff open. Reverse stitch at either side of the turning gap and over the hanging loop for extra strength (see page 24). Trim the seam allowance to $^3/_{16}$in (5mm), apart from at the turning gap.

9 Turn the outer piece right side out and tack the pompom trim around the top edge of the cuff, turning the ends up and over the raw edge where you start and finish.

10 With the cuff and lining piece still inside out, slip the outer piece inside it.

11 Push the outer piece snugly down inside the lining so that the top edges and their seams align. Pin or tack around the top before stitching a $^3/_8$in (1cm) seam. Turn your work right sides out through the turning gap. Tuck the raw edges in at the gap, pin together and close by hand using overstitch (see page 16).

12 Push the outer piece snugly down inside the lining and cuff piece. Press. Pin or tack through all layers along the seam joining the cuff to the lining. Topstitch along here $^1/_8$in (3mm) to the cuff side of the seam. Turn your work right sides out and push the lining right down inside the outer piece.

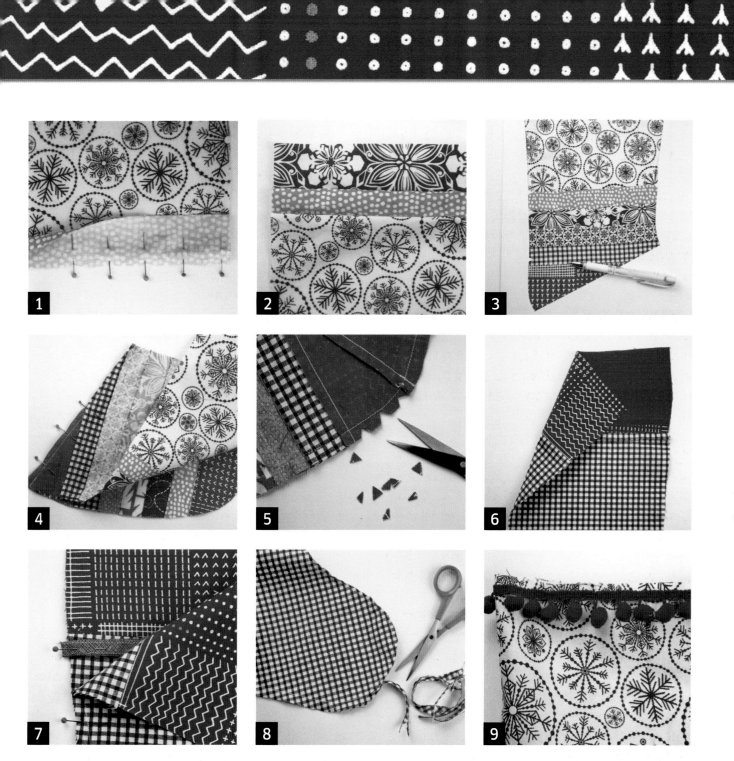

# WRAPPING
# IT UP

# GIFT TAG

This smart, hardwearing gift tag is a present in itself, as a traditional luggage label in floral and patterned fabric. This project is a bit fiddly the first time you make one, but once you're in the rhythm, you can make them very quickly and efficiently.

Find the templates on page 146

You will need
7 x 12in (18 x 30cm) of fabric
6 x 10in (10 x 26cm) of fusible interfacing
3 x 5in (8 x 12.5cm) of fusible stabilizer
¾in (18mm) eyelet and fixing kit
Clear plastic file or wallet for your label 'window'
Tracing paper or baking parchment
Pencil
Paper-cutting scissors
Sewing machine
Thread to match fabric
Pins
Sharp scissors
Air-erasable pen or tailor's chalk
Iron

NOTE: One fat quarter will make three tags.

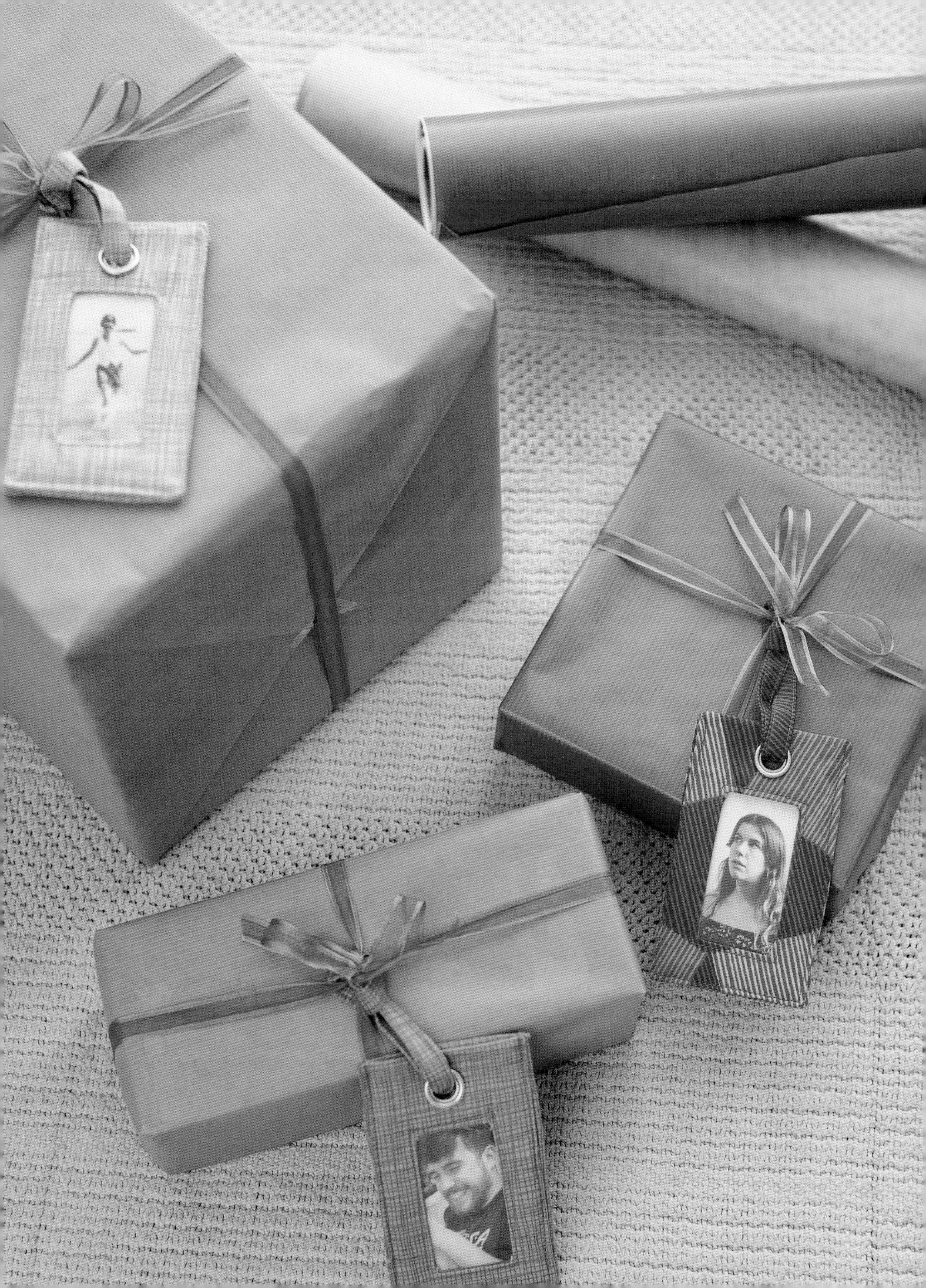

1 Use the templates on page 146 to cut out four rectangles of fabric, two pieces of interfacing and one of stabilizer. Fix one piece of interfacing to the wrong side of one rectangle of fabric, leaving a ³/₁₆in (5mm) seam allowance all the way around. Repeat with a second rectangle of fabric and place these two pieces right sides together. Pin or tack together. Sew a ³/₁₆in (5mm) seam using the edge of the interfacing as a guide for the stitch line.

2 Draw the cutting lines on one side of your work, referring to the template on page 146. Note that the rectangle for the window edge lies 1in (2.5cm) from three edges, but 1¹/₂in (4cm) from one short end. Use sharp scissors to cut the 'X' through both layers of fabric.

3 Fold the four triangles created by the cut 'X' out and away from the centre of your work using the drawn rectangle as guidelines for the folds. Press the folds with a hot iron.

4 Trim the excess fabric ³/₁₆in (5mm) from the fold edges. Turn the work over and repeat this folding and trimming process. Clip all corners diagonally (see page 27).

5 Turn right sides out through the central 'window'. There may be fraying at the corners – trim with small, sharp scissors. Use a pin to pick at the four corners, making them as sharp as possible before pressing your work.

6 Cut a piece of clear plastic 3 x 1³/₄in (7.5 x 4.5cm) and slip it in between the two layers of fabric that form your 'window frame'.

7 Top stitch (see page 21) round the window, ¹/₈in (3mm) from the edge through all layers of fabric and plastic. Leave the needle down at each corner, raise the foot and pivot your work before lowering it again and stitching along to the next corner. Insert an eyelet as indicated on the template, following the instructions on the kit (see page 27).

8 Fix the piece of stabilizer to the centre of the wrong side of one of your two remaining rectangles of fabric. Place these two pieces of fabric right sides together and pin or tack together. Sew a ³/₁₆in (5mm) seam all the way round, stitching just beyond the edge of the stabilizer and leaving the turning gap along one edge as indicated on the template. Clip the corners diagonally.

9 Turn your work right sides out through the turning gap. Tease the seams and pick at the corners with a pin to make them sharp. Fold the raw edges in at the gap. Press and close the turning gap by hand with overstitch (see page 16).

10 Make a hanging loop from a 10in (25cm) piece of fabric following the instructions on page 27. Fold it in half, aligning the raw ends. Carefully snip a little slot ³/₈in (1cm) from one short end of your label back through just one layer of fabric as marked on the template. Slot the raw ends of your hanging loop in by about ³/₈in (1cm). Use zigzag stitch to anchor the hanging loop securely.

11 Place your 'window' on top of the back piece, slot the loop through the eyelet and align the edges. Leaving the hanging loop end open, top stitch around the remaining three sides ¹/₈in (3mm) from the edge, starting and finishing with reverse stitching (see page 24).

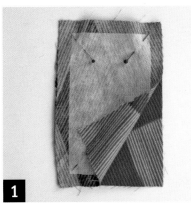

1

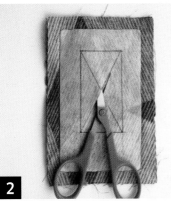

9

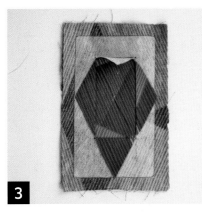

10

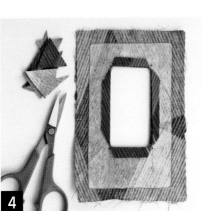

8

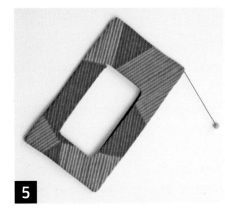

7

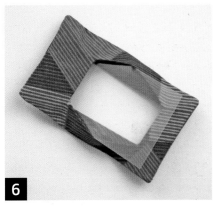

3

6

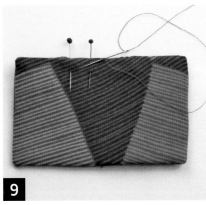

5

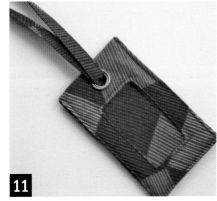

4

11

# BOTTLE COOL BAG

A thermal-lined bottle bag keeps a gift of wine or bubbly chilled and makes a special extra present, which can be re-used months later on summer picnics. This is a good snug fit for a standard wine-bottle size with a 10in (25.5cm) diameter at its widest.

Find the templates on page 147

You will need
1 fat quarter of outer fabric
1 fat quarter of lining fabric
15 x 16¼in (38 x 41cm) of thermal wadding
15in (38cm) length of ¾in (2cm)-wide bias binding
Tracing paper or baking parchment
Pencil
Paper-cutting scissors
Sewing machine
Thread to match fabric
Sewing needle
Pins
Sharp scissors
Air-erasable pen or tailor's chalk
Iron

NOTE: You need to cut out a 4¼in (11cm) square each of outer fabric, lining fabric and thermal wadding for the base before you start the project.

## Tip
*Some sparkling wines have wider bottles so you may need to adjust the width, the size of the base circle and the length of bias binding accordingly.*

1 Use the template on page 147 to cut out the side pieces. Place one rectangle of outer fabric and one of lining fabric right sides together, aligning the raw edges. With the lining side facing you, use the template to mark the top edge and the handle on the fabric. Stitch along the marked handle line by machine – take this really slowly, raising and lowering the foot with the needle down through the fabric now and again to achieve smooth curves at either end.

2 Use sharp scissors to cut away the inside of the handle, leaving a $^3/_{16}$in (5mm) seam allowance around the stitch line. Make small cuts into this around the handle hole, taking great care not to snip the stitches (see page 27).

3 Turn your work right sides out by pulling the outer fabric out through the handle hole.

4 Tweak and tease the edge of the handle hole to make it as neat and crisp as possible while aligning the raw edges of fabric. Press with a hot iron. Use the template to mark the curved top edge of your bag again.

5 Take one rectangle of thermal wadding and use the template on page 147 to mark out and cut out the handle hole. Note that this hole is slightly bigger than the one for the outer and lining – this allows space for the seam allowance and avoids puckering around it. Feed the lining layer through the handle hole cut in the wadding so that the wadding is now sandwiched between the two layers of fabric. Tweak the three layers until they lie as flat as possible and the raw edges are aligned. The edges may be slightly uneven but do the best you can to even them out. Pin or tack all the way round before top stitching $^3/_{16}$in (5mm) in from the edge (see page 21). Trim the seam close to the line of top stitching.

6 Repeat steps 1–5 to create the bag's second side. Place the two padded sides right sides together and pin or tack along the two long side edges. Machine stitch $^1/_4$in (6mm) seams along each edge. Choose a thread that blends well with the lining fabric to bind the raw side seam edges with a wide and very close zigzag stitch.

7 Use the base template on page 147 to cut out the lining fabric and thermal wadding. Lay the lining fabric wrong side down on the wadding, then place these two layers down on to the wrong side of the 4$^1/_4$in (11cm) square of outer fabric. Pin or tack the three layers together before top stitching $^3/_{16}$in (5mm) inside the edge of the circle. Trim the excess outer fabric to leave a neat circle of wadding sandwiched between the outer and lining fabrics.

8 With the body of the bag still inside out, carefully pin or tack the circle to fit snugly to the bottom raw edge, right sides together. Sew a $^1/_4$in (6mm) seam round this edge by machine – work slowly to minimize puckering and achieve as smooth a stitched seam as possible.

9 Repeat the zigzag stitching from step 6 to finish off the raw edges of this circular seam.

10 Turn your work right side out. Open the bias binding out and pin or tack it right sides together along the bag's top raw edge. Fold the leading edge of the bias binding $^1/_4$in (6mm) towards you and lay the finishing end over this fold before trimming it, overlapping the initial fold by $^3/_8$in (1cm). Stitch along the top crease of the tape through all layers.

11 Turn the bag inside out again. Fold the binding over to encase the raw edge and sew down by hand using hem stitch (see page 16).

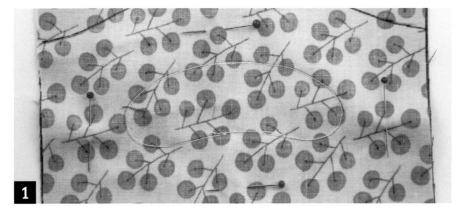

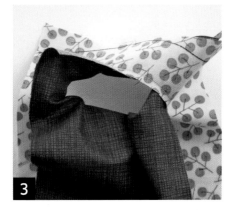

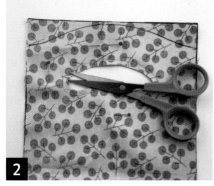

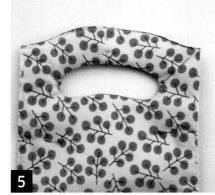

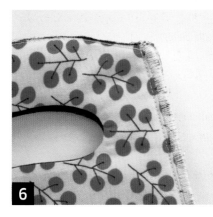

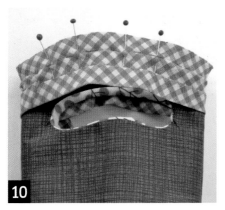

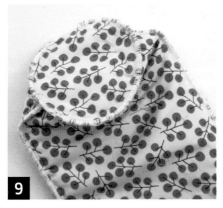

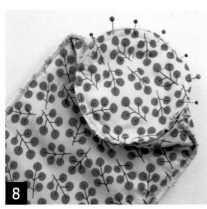

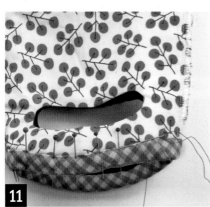

# PARCEL ROSETTE

Embellish your gift-wrapping with a beautiful fabric rosette made from single or assorted fabrics. It could even be worn as a pretty corsage, or as a smart addition to a hat or bag. Make several: they look fantastic as a decorative bouquet clustered on a parcel.

You will need
(makes one rosette)
½ fat quarter of fabric
11 x 11in (28 x 28cm) of fusible interfacing
1³/₈ x 1³/₈in (3.5 x 3.5cm) of heavy stabilizer
A6 piece of thin card
Drawing compass and pencil
Paper-cutting scissors
1 x safety pin or brooch clip
Sewing machine
Thread to match fabric
Sewing needle
Pins
Sharp scissors
Air-erasable pen or tailor's chalk
Iron

NOTE: One fat quarter will make three rosettes.

1 Make templates by using the compass to draw two circles on the card, one with a diameter of 3½in (9cm) and the other 1⅜in (3.5cm). Cut out with paper-cutting scissors. Draw around the larger template to cut out ten circles of fabric and nine of fusible interfacing. Use the small template to cut out one circle of heavy stabilizer. Take one circle of fabric and, using the thread doubled, sew 3/16in (5mm) running stitches 3/16in (5mm) in from the edge all the way around. Keep the needle and thread attached.

2 With the wrong side of this piece of fabric facing up, place the small circle of stabilizer in the centre of it, then pull the needle and thread to gather the outer edge of the fabric and draw it into the centre, completely enclosing the stabilizer. Make a few firm stitches to finish off and secure the gathering.

3 Prepare the remaining nine circles. For each circle, use an iron to fuse the interfacing to the wrong side of the fabric.

4 Take one circle and fold it in half, wrong sides together, aligning the raw edges. Now fold this semi-circle into thirds and machine stitch back and forth across the point a few times to hold the folds – this will be the central 'petal' of the rosette. Take one of the remaining eight circles and fold it in half, wrong sides together, aligning the raw edges. Now fold this semi-circle in half again and stitch back and forth across the point a few times by machine to hold the folds. Repeat this with the remaining seven circles.

5 With the gathered side of the small circle facing up, take one of the eight petals folded into quarters from step 4. Using the thread doubled, hand sew it with overstitch (see page 16) about 3/16in (5mm) along either side of the fold point so that the tip meets the centre of the small covered circle. Do the same with three more petals, at the same time making sure that they are all placed with their folds positioned in the same direction.

6 Repeat step 5 with the next four petals, but this time, place them so that their folds are positioned in the opposite direction to the previous four. At the same time, stitch them down at 45 degrees to the previous layer – each 'petal' centred over the join between two on the previous layer.

7 Take the remaining central petal from step 4, and stitch it to the centre of the rosette. Finish off the thread.

8 Turn the work over and use over stitch to sew the circle of fabric to the first layer of petals, taking care to pick up and stitch through one layer of fabric only.

9 Finally, stitch a safety pin (or brooch clip) to the centre of the back of your rosette.

## Tip

*This rosette can be easily re-sized by making it from smaller or larger circles of fabric.*

1

2

3

4

5

6

7

8

9

# PARCEL BELT

A narrow strip of fabric makes a belt to wrap a parcel – and creates an extra gift at the same time. Pick up old belts in thrift shops for vintage buckles; they also come in a huge variety of designs and colours from haberdashery stores or online.

Find the template on page 146

You will need
1 x belt buckle
1 piece of fabric twice the inside measurement of the belt bar, plus ¾in (2cm) by as long as you want your belt to be – it will need to be at least 6in (15cm) longer than the parcel's circumference
Cotton embroidery thread to match fabric
Embroidery needle
1 x 4mm (UK8:US6) knitting needle
Embroidery needle
Sewing machine
Thread to match fabric
Sewing needle
Pins
Sharp scissors
Air-erasable pen or tailor's chalk
Iron

NOTE: One fat quarter will make two belts. Join several strips with ⅜in (1cm) seams pressed flat to make up the length of fabric you require.

1 Fold the piece of fabric (wrong sides together) in half lengthways and align the long raw edges. Pin or tack before making a point at one end, referring to the template on page 146. Your point will be at 45 degrees to the long edge and turn 90 degrees at its tip. Remember to take into account the $^3/8$in (1cm) seam allowance along the long edge – it's worth marking this before marking the pointed end. Stitch around the marked, pointed end twice for strength, and then sew a $^3/8$in (1cm) seam along the long edge, reversing as you finish (see page 24) and leaving the short end open for turning.

2 Snip the excess fabric around the pointed end with sharp scissors, taking great care not to cut too close to the stitch line.

3 Use a blunt tool such as a knitting needle to turn the work right sides out through the unstitched end.

4 Use a pin to pick at the tip of the pointed end to make it sharp. Tease and manipulate the long seam of your work to make it neat and even before pressing the whole thing with a hot iron.

5 Lay the buckle 2–2½in (5–6.25cm) from the open end of the belt and mark a point where the buckle pin hinges on its bar.

6 Push the end of a knitting needle through both layers of fabric at the marked position from step 5. You need to push it through to separate the threads of the fabric, but not to break them. Make this 'hole' just big enough to push the embroidery needle through a couple of times – it will stretch slightly larger as you work. Thread the needle with embroidery cotton and, working in a circle, hand sew $^1/8$in (3mm) overstitches (see page 16) around the edge of the hole to create an eyelet buttonhole.

7 Push the buckle pin through the buttonhole – you may need to tease it larger with the knitting needle again to accommodate the pin's width. Make sure you have the buckle the right way round when you thread the belt on to it.

8 Turn your work over – wrong side up – and trim the raw end of the fabric to 1in (2.5cm) from the buckle pin. Tuck the raw end of the fabric under by ¼in (6mm) and stitch down securely by hand using hem stitch (see page 16) and with the thread doubled for extra strength.

9 At the pointed end, mark three or more points 1½in (4cm) apart and starting 2in (5cm) from your belt's tip. Stitch eyelet buttonholes at each point as in step 6.

# Tip

*A quicker version of this can be made by using a strip of velvet or taffeta ribbon and skipping steps 1–5.*

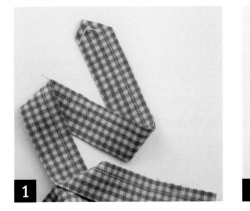

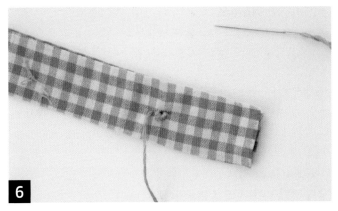

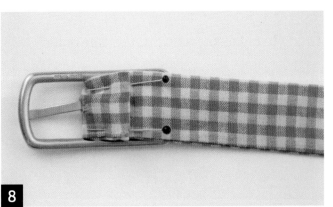

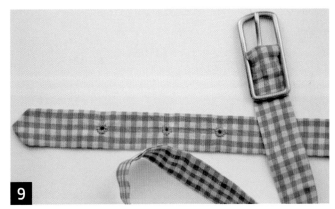

# GIFT BAG

A very smart way to wrap presents, this lined bag doubles up as a bonus gift. With a little confidence, you can make a customized bag for any present. Do a mock-up first with a single layer of paper, using tape or a stapler for the seams, to create a template.

Find the templates on page 146

You will need
(for a bag measuring 8½ x 3½ x 3in [21.5 x 9 x 7.5cm])
½ fat quarter of outer fabric
½ fat quarter of lining fabric
12½ x 10in (32 x 25cm) of fusible interfacing
2 x buttons, ⅝in (1.5cm) and ½in (12mm) in diameter
12in (30cm) of cotton embroidery thread or crochet thread
Scrap of pompom trim or a small amount of knitting yarn
    to make your own small pompom
Tracing paper or baking parchment
Sewing machine
Thread to match fabric
Sewing needle
Paper-cutting scissors
Pencil
Pins
Sharp scissors
Air-erasable pen or tailor's chalk
Knitting needle or other blunt tool (optional)
Iron

NOTE: One fat quarter will make one bag with the same outer and lining fabric.

1 Use the template on page 146 to cut out the outer fabric, lining and interfacing. Fuse interfacing to the wrong side of both pieces of the outer fabric, centring each piece of interfacing to leave a 3/8in (1cm) seam allowance all the way round. Now place these two pieces of fabric right sides together. Align the raw edges and pin along the two long sides and one short edge. Stitch a 3/8in (1cm) seam round these three edges.

2 Do the same with the lining fabric, only this time leave a turning gap along one long edge, as indicated on the template.

3 Clip the two bottom corners of the outer and lining pieces diagonally with small, sharp scissors (see page 27).

4 Press the seams on both pieces of work. Fold the seam allowance back upon itself on each side so that it lies towards the centre of your work and over the interfacing.

5 Turn the outer piece right sides out before slotting it inside the lining piece.

6 Push the outer fabric snugly down inside the lining so that the raw top edges align. Pin or tack round this edge before machine stitching a 3/8in (1cm) seam.

7 Pull the work right sides out through the turning gap in the lining.

8 Fold the raw edges in at the turning gap. Pin or tack the sides of the gap together before closing it by hand using overstitch (see page 16).

9 Push the lining down inside the outer fabric. Use your fingers or a blunt tool such as a knitting needle to prod the two bottom corners to ensure the layers of fabric fit snugly together.

10 Following the instructions on page 23 and using the template on page 146, create two box corners.

11 Sew the larger button on the outside of the bag, 4in (10cm) from the top edge.

12 Turn the bag over and anchor one end of the embroidery cotton 1in (2.5cm) from the top edge with a few overlapping stitches before covering this point with the smaller button. Stitch a small ready-made pompom to the other end of the embroidery thread.

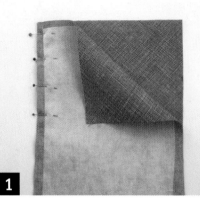

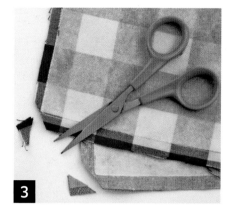

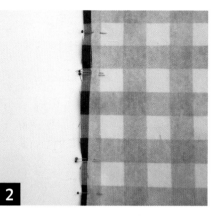

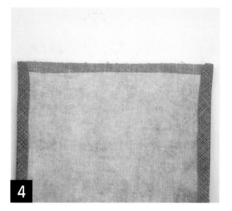

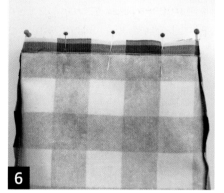

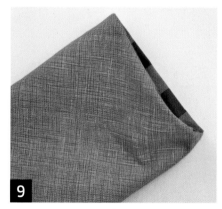

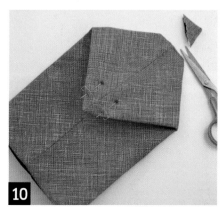

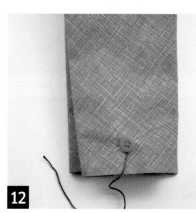

# TEMPLATES

Templates that are shown at actual size can be traced and cut out, or photocopied.
For templates that have been reduced in size, enlarge them on an A3 photocopier
to the percentage stated on the pattern pieces.

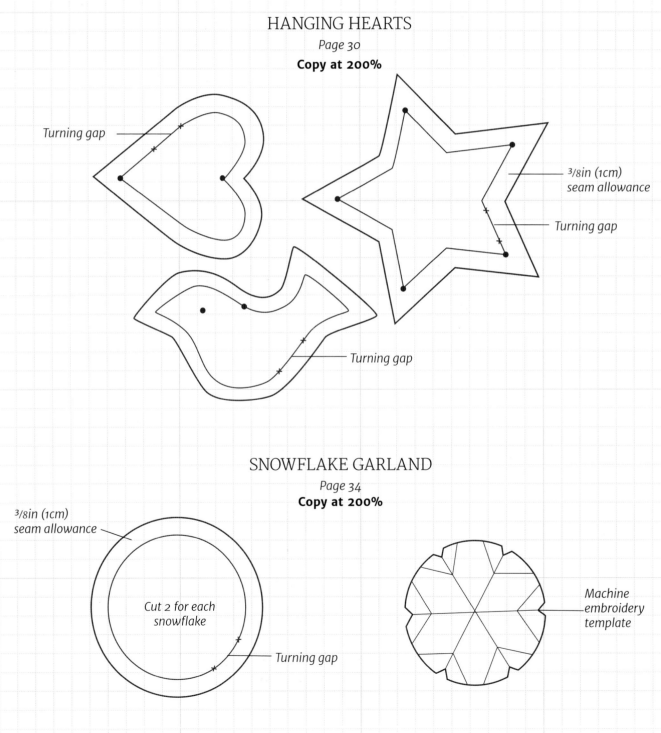

## HANGING HEARTS
*Page 30*
**Copy at 200%**

Turning gap

³/8in (1cm)
seam allowance

Turning gap

Turning gap

## SNOWFLAKE GARLAND
*Page 34*
**Copy at 200%**

³/8in (1cm)
seam allowance

Cut 2 for each
snowflake

Turning gap

Machine
embroidery
template

# TREE BUNTING
*Page 38*
**Copy at 100%**

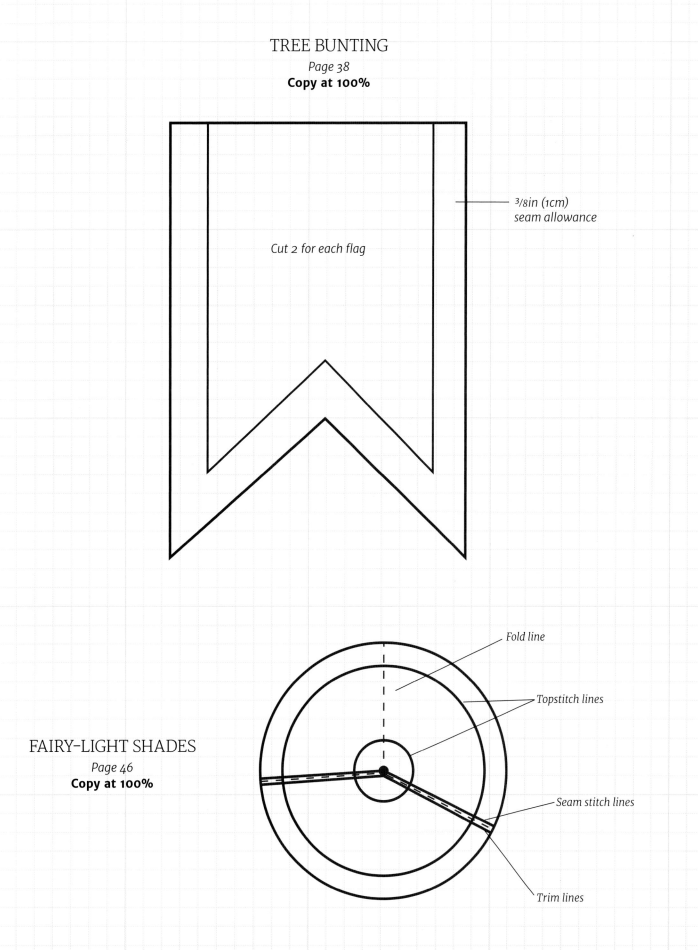

3/8in (1cm)
seam allowance

Cut 2 for each flag

Fold line

Topstitch lines

# FAIRY-LIGHT SHADES
*Page 46*
**Copy at 100%**

Seam stitch lines

Trim lines

# WINTER TREE
*Page 52*
**Copy at 200%**

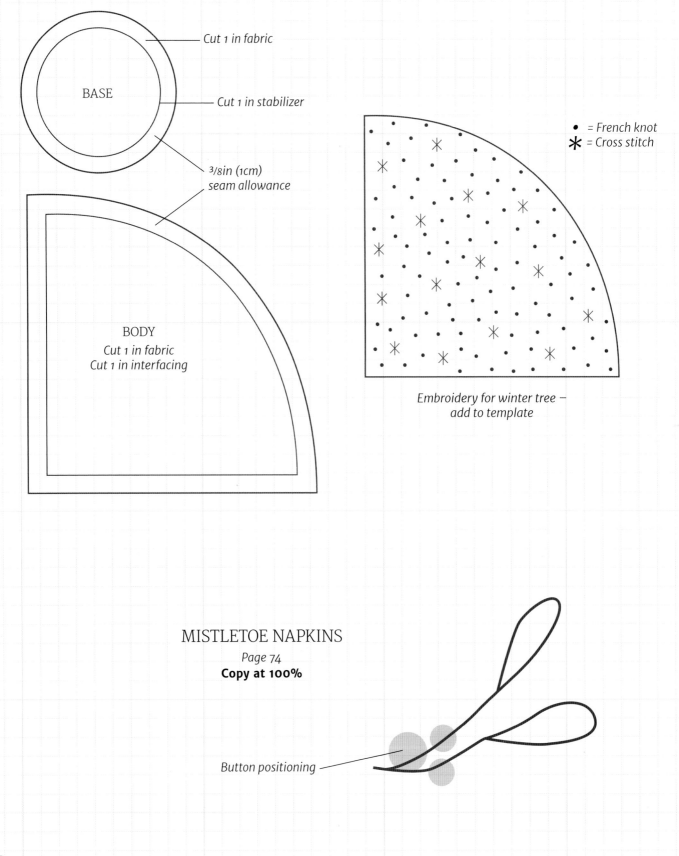

BASE

Cut 1 in fabric

Cut 1 in stabilizer

³/8in (1cm)
seam allowance

BODY
*Cut 1 in fabric*
*Cut 1 in interfacing*

• = French knot
✱ = Cross stitch

*Embroidery for winter tree –
add to template*

# MISTLETOE NAPKINS
*Page 74*
**Copy at 100%**

Button positioning

# WINTER HOUSE
*Page 56*
**Copy at 200%**

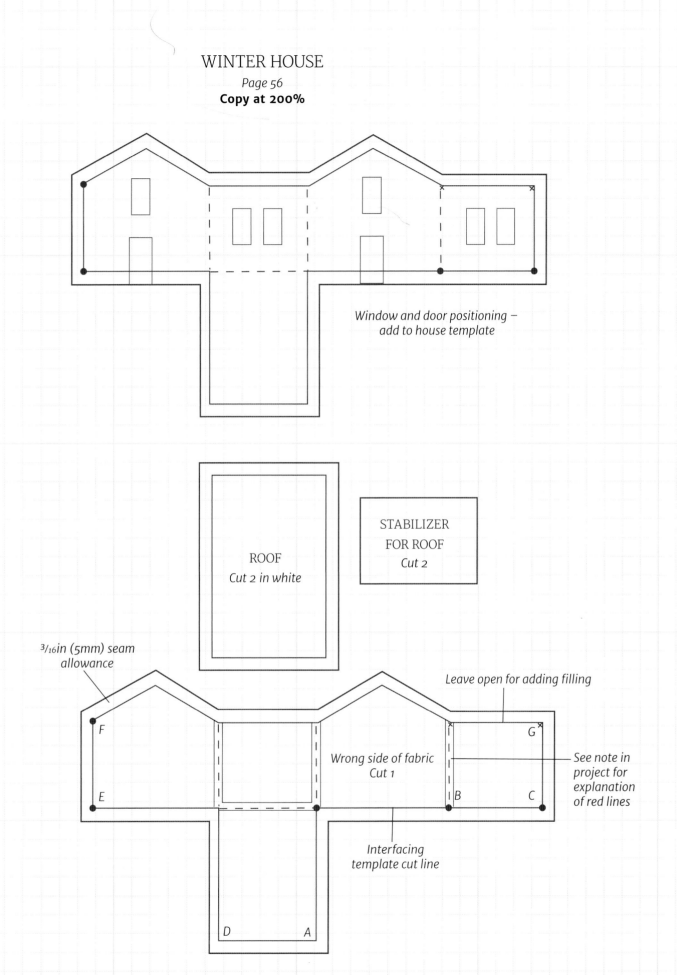

Window and door positioning –
add to house template

ROOF
*Cut 2 in white*

STABILIZER
FOR ROOF
*Cut 2*

*³/₁₆in (5mm) seam
allowance*

F

E

*Wrong side of fabric
Cut 1*

*Leave open for adding filling*

G

B          C

*See note in
project for
explanation
of red lines*

*Interfacing
template cut line*

D          A

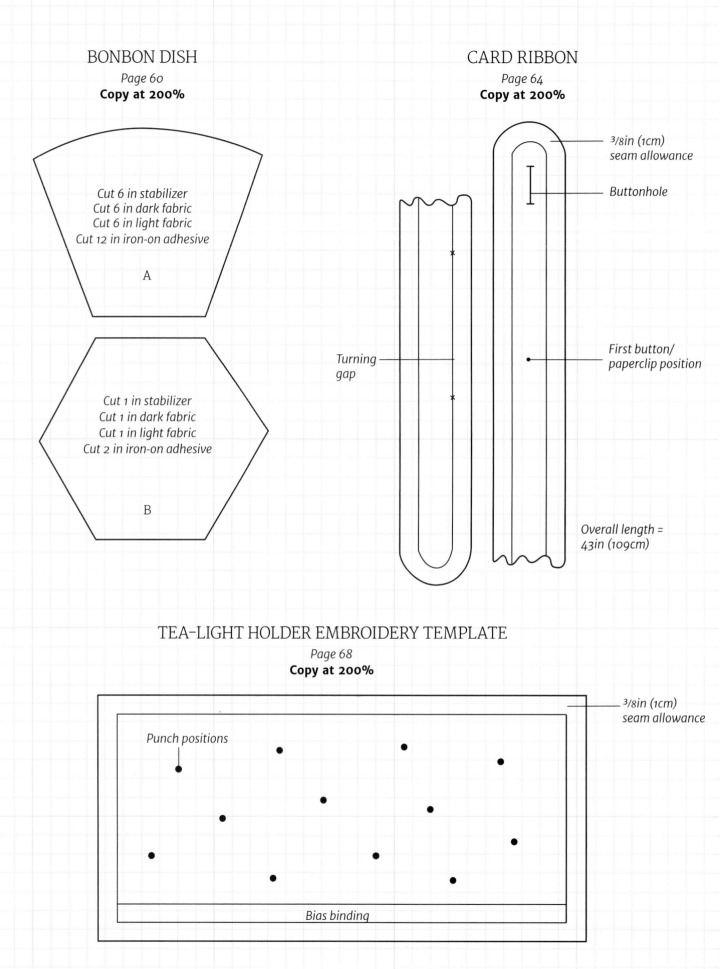

## BONBON DISH

*Page 60*
**Copy at 200%**

Cut 6 in stabilizer
Cut 6 in dark fabric
Cut 6 in light fabric
Cut 12 in iron-on adhesive

A

Cut 1 in stabilizer
Cut 1 in dark fabric
Cut 1 in light fabric
Cut 2 in iron-on adhesive

B

## CARD RIBBON

*Page 64*
**Copy at 200%**

³/8in (1cm)
seam allowance

Buttonhole

Turning gap

First button/
paperclip position

Overall length =
43in (109cm)

## TEA-LIGHT HOLDER EMBROIDERY TEMPLATE

*Page 68*
**Copy at 200%**

³/8in (1cm)
seam allowance

Punch positions

Bias binding

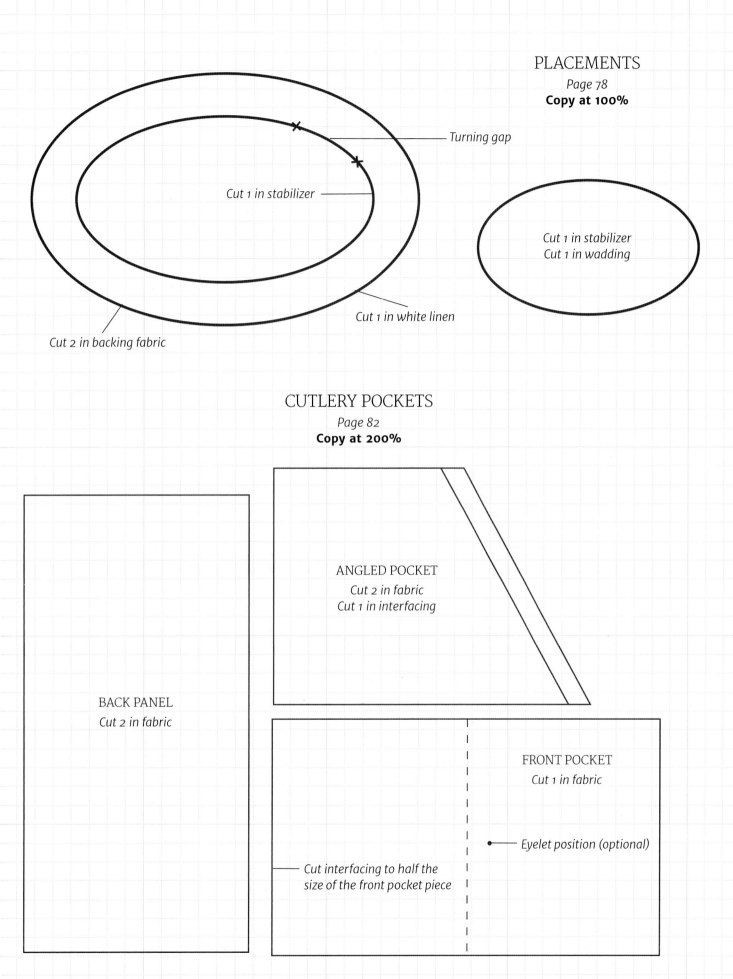

# PLACEMENTS
*Page 78*
**Copy at 100%**

Turning gap

Cut 1 in stabilizer

Cut 1 in white linen

Cut 2 in backing fabric

Cut 1 in stabilizer
Cut 1 in wadding

# CUTLERY POCKETS
*Page 82*
**Copy at 200%**

ANGLED POCKET
*Cut 2 in fabric*
*Cut 1 in interfacing*

BACK PANEL
*Cut 2 in fabric*

FRONT POCKET
*Cut 1 in fabric*

Eyelet position (optional)

Cut interfacing to half the
size of the front pocket piece

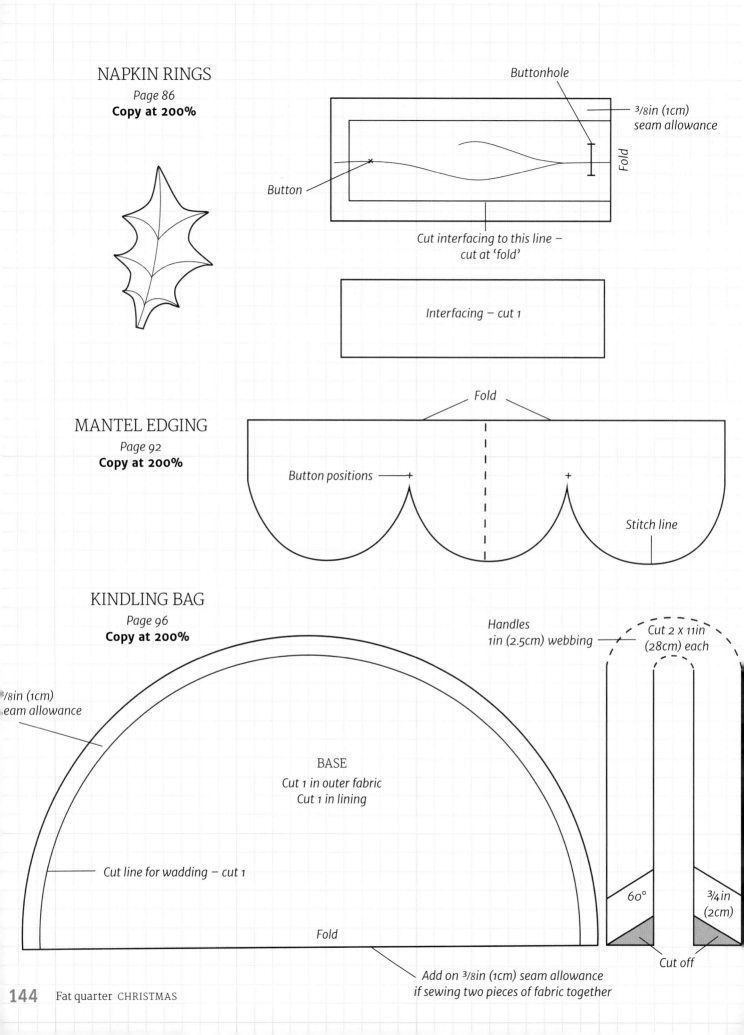

## NAPKIN RINGS

*Page 86*
**Copy at 200%**

Buttonhole

³/8in (1cm)
seam allowance

Fold

Button

Cut interfacing to this line –
cut at 'fold'

Interfacing – cut 1

## MANTEL EDGING

*Page 92*
**Copy at 200%**

Fold

Button positions +

+

Stitch line

## KINDLING BAG

*Page 96*
**Copy at 200%**

³/8in (1cm)
seam allowance

BASE
Cut 1 in outer fabric
Cut 1 in lining

Cut line for wadding – cut 1

Fold

Add on ³/8in (1cm) seam allowance
if sewing two pieces of fabric together

Handles
1in (2.5cm) webbing

Cut 2 x 11in
(28cm) each

60°

³/4in
(2cm)

Cut off

# SPILL HOLDER

*Page 100*
**Copy at 200%**

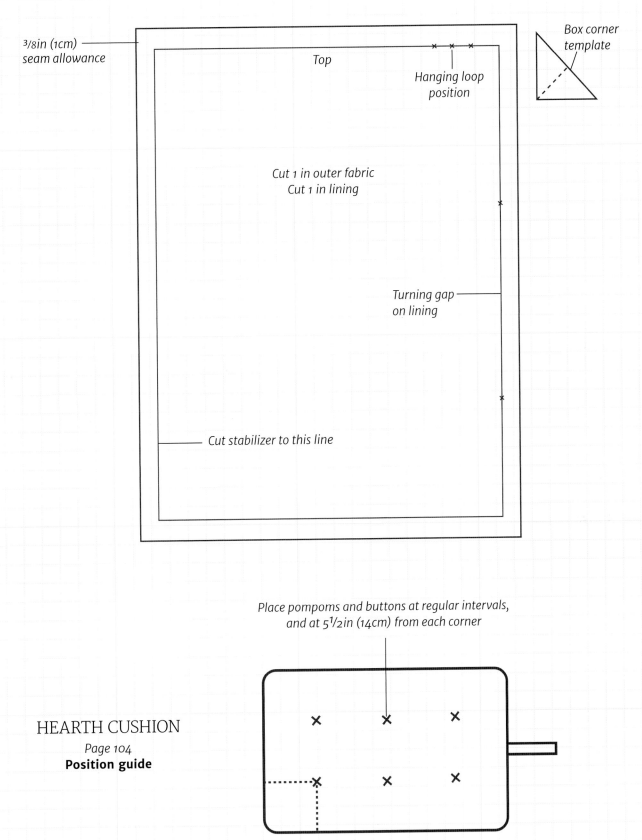

3/8in (1cm)
seam allowance

Top

Hanging loop
position

Box corner
template

Cut 1 in outer fabric
Cut 1 in lining

Turning gap
on lining

Cut stabilizer to this line

Place pompoms and buttons at regular intervals,
and at 5¹/₂in (14cm) from each corner

# HEARTH CUSHION

*Page 104*
**Position guide**

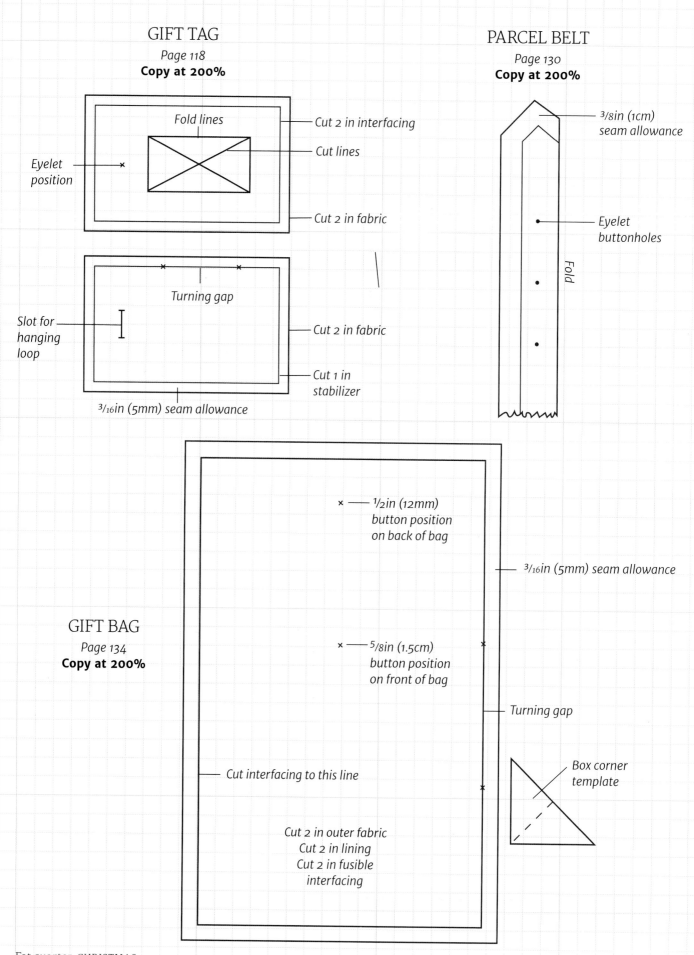

## GIFT TAG
*Page 118*
**Copy at 200%**

Fold lines

Eyelet position

Cut 2 in interfacing

Cut lines

Cut 2 in fabric

Turning gap

Slot for hanging loop

Cut 2 in fabric

Cut 1 in stabilizer

³/₁₆in (5mm) seam allowance

## PARCEL BELT
*Page 130*
**Copy at 200%**

³/₈in (1cm) seam allowance

Eyelet buttonholes

Fold

## GIFT BAG
*Page 134*
**Copy at 200%**

× — ½in (12mm) button position on back of bag

³/₁₆in (5mm) seam allowance

× — ⁵/₈in (1.5cm) button position on front of bag

Turning gap

Cut interfacing to this line

Box corner template

Cut 2 in outer fabric
Cut 2 in lining
Cut 2 in fusible interfacing

# BOTTLE COOL BAG

*Page 122*
**Copy at 200%**

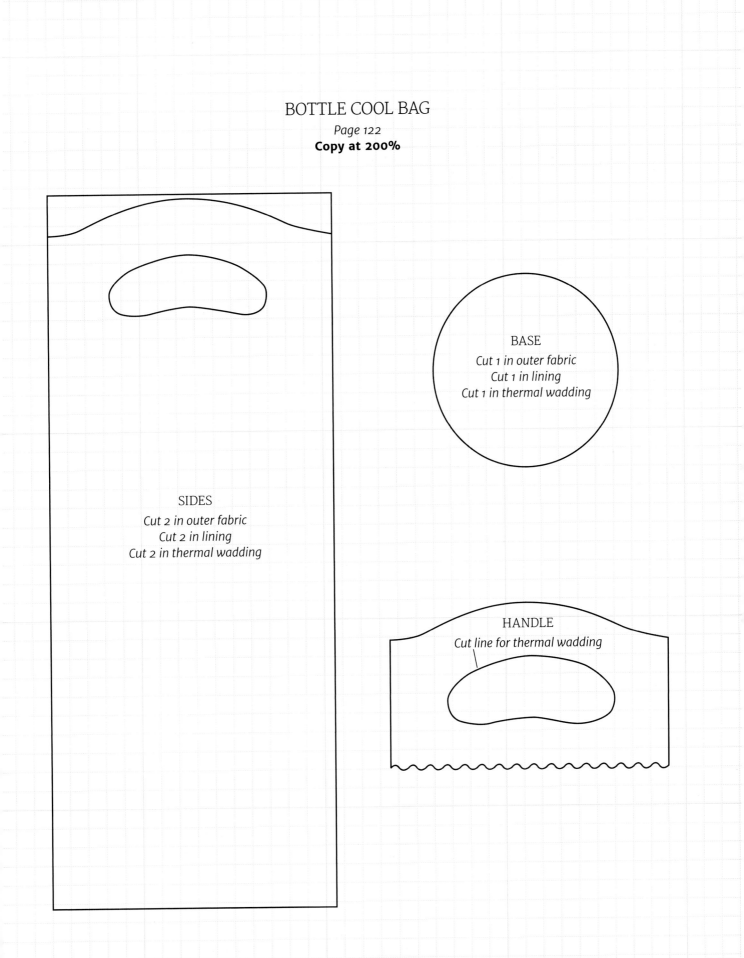

SIDES

*Cut 2 in outer fabric*
*Cut 2 in lining*
*Cut 2 in thermal wadding*

BASE

*Cut 1 in outer fabric*
*Cut 1 in lining*
*Cut 1 in thermal wadding*

HANDLE

*Cut line for thermal wadding*

# TRADITIONAL AND STRIPED STOCKINGS
### Pages 108 and 112
### Copy at 250%

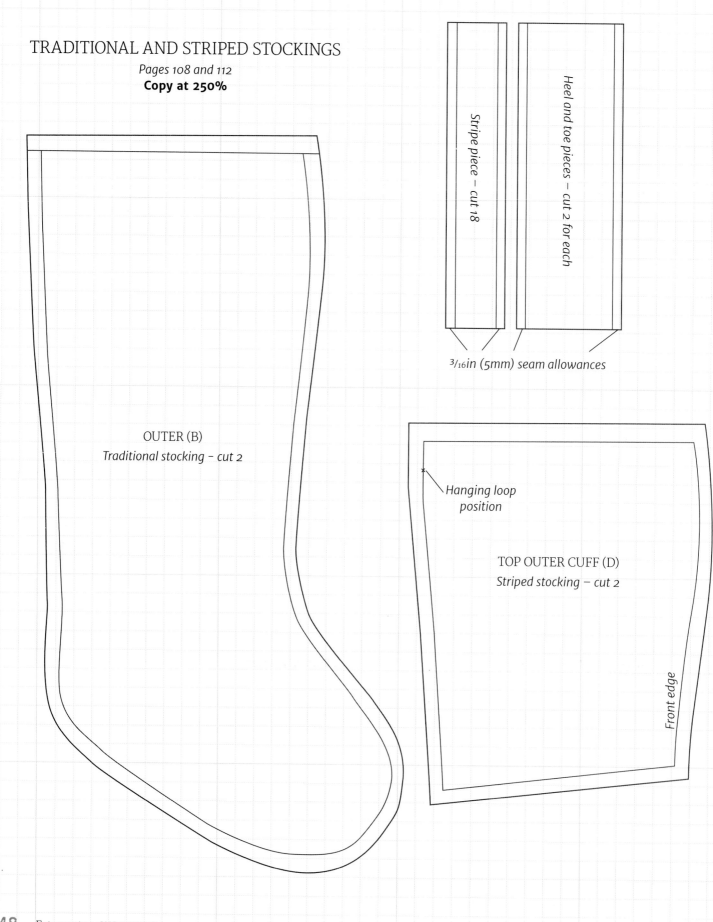

Stripe piece – cut 18

Heel and toe pieces – cut 2 for each

³/₁₆in (5mm) seam allowances

OUTER (B)
*Traditional stocking – cut 2*

*Hanging loop position*

TOP OUTER CUFF (D)
*Striped stocking – cut 2*

*Front edge*

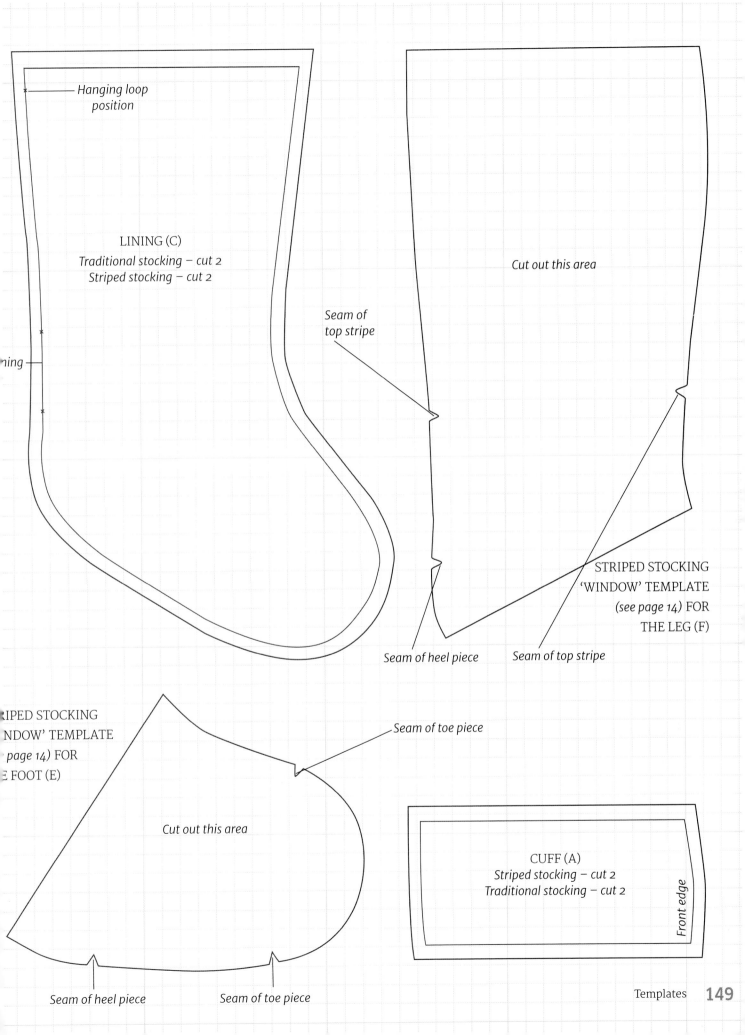

Hanging loop position

LINING (C)
Traditional stocking – cut 2
Striped stocking – cut 2

...ning

Seam of top stripe

Cut out this area

Seam of top stripe

STRIPED STOCKING 'WINDOW' TEMPLATE
(see page 14) FOR THE LEG (F)

Seam of heel piece

Seam of toe piece

...IPED STOCKING
...NDOW' TEMPLATE
...page 14) FOR
...FOOT (E)

Cut out this area

Seam of heel piece

Seam of toe piece

CUFF (A)
Striped stocking – cut 2
Traditional stocking – cut 2

Front edge

# RESOURCES

Fabrics, wadding, interfacing, stabilizers etc
**The Village Haberdashery**
www.thevillagehaberdashery.co.uk

Haberdashery and scissors
**The Brighton Sewing Centre**
www.brightonsewingcentre.co.uk

Bells, fairy lights
**Amazon**
www.amazon.co.uk

Yarn
**Erika Knight**
www.erikaknight.co.uk

Sewing machine
**Janome**
www.janome.co.uk

# ACKNOWLEDGEMENTS

A big thank you to Emma Sekhon for the wonderful photography, as ever. To Gilda, Luana, Jonathan, Robin, Sara and everyone at GMC for their input. Erika for her delicious yarns. Glenn for his persistent skills and care. My friends and, above all, my lovely family, especially Harrison and Martha.

# INDEX

To order a book, or to request
a catalogue, contact:

GMC Publications Ltd
Castle Place, 166 High Street,
Lewes, East Sussex,
BN7 1XU
United Kingdom
Tel: +44 (0)1273 488005
www.gmcbooks.com